INDIANAPOLIS
JAZZ

INDIANAPOLIS
JAZZ

The Masters,
Legends and
Legacy of
Indiana Avenue

DAVID LEANDER
WILLIAMS

Foreword by David N. Baker

Charleston   London

THE
History
PRESS

Published by The History Press
Charleston, SC 29403
www.historypress.net

Top middle image on back cover courtesy of Larry Goshen.

Images courtesy of the author unless otherwise noted.

First published 2014

Manufactured in the United States

ISBN 978.1.62619.403.8

Library of Congress CIP data applied for.

This book is dedicated to the memory of my parents and relatives:

Lomax Mahone, Emogene Carson-Williams-Mahone, Claude Deon Williams, Jessie Carson, Betty Jean Williams, Jessica Georgianne Williams, Rudd Kenneth Williams and Susie Yvonne Williams.

"Love Supreme."

Contents

Foreword

New Orleans. Chicago. New York. Kansas City. These cities are among those immediately recognized as major centers of importance in the history of jazz. Their stories have been well documented and are familiar to aficionados and scholars alike.

But there are a number of other American cities whose musicians, venues and populations have also made significant contributions to the fabric of jazz history and whose stories have yet to be told. One of these cities is Indianapolis, Indiana.

I was born in Indianapolis in 1931, and its story is one I know well. Although segregation was the order of the day at that time, the black community in which I grew up had a long and rich history. I am a proud product of such legendary institutions as Crispus Attucks High School—at that time an all-black high school that would come to count among its graduates many notables in the arts, sciences, business, athletics and the military—Eastern Star Baptist Church and the Indianapolis jazz scene, of which Indiana Avenue was the acknowledged center.

Historically, in many cities with a large urban black population, there was an area in which the principal businesses, restaurants, theaters, clubs and other buildings/venues of importance were located. Within this area there was often a street or boulevard of particular prominence. For the black community of Indianapolis, that street was Indiana Avenue.

The story of Indiana Avenue was a book I had thought I might someday write myself. This street was the heart and soul of the Indianapolis I knew, and as a musician who came of age on the Avenue, performed there off and on for many years and knew much of the history and many of the musicians firsthand, I knew it was an extraordinary story that needed to be told and told by someone who knew it intimately.

Indianapolis Jazz: The Masters, Legends and Legacy of Indiana Avenue is that book, and David Williams is the perfect person to have written it.

David is a dear friend and fellow graduate of Crispus Attucks High School. He is exceptionally knowledgeable about many things, including the history of Indiana Avenue and the city of Indianapolis, and especially that of its black community. In this work, he skillfully combines decades of painstaking research with his personal experiences and acquaintance with the subject matter about which he has written. In doing so, he has created an authentic and thoroughly entertaining portrait of this legendary street and the people and places responsible for its greatness.

Not much has been written to date about the rich history of Indianapolis's black community. *Indianapolis Jazz: The Masters, Legends and Legacy of Indiana Avenue* is significant not only in that it documents an important part of that history but also because it is the work of a black historian writing about the people, places and activities of his own community.

This book is both a valuable contribution to scholarship and a delight to read. Thank you, David Williams, for your passion and perseverance in telling and preserving this historically significant and fascinating story.

DAVID N. BAKER
Chairman Emeritus, Jazz Studies Department, Indiana University Jacobs School of Music, Bloomington, Indiana
Conductor Emeritus, Smithsonian Jazz Masterworks Orchestra, Washington, D.C.
National Endowment for the Arts American Jazz Master
John F. Kennedy Center for the Performing Arts Living Jazz Legend

Reflections on the Avenue

As I think back over my more than seventy years in music, I really feel so fortunate that my journey has been a pleasant one. It certainly has been an awe-inspiring one. I was blessed to have two of the greatest music educators one could ask for in my parents, Clark Hampton and Laura Burford-Hampton. My mother and father instructed and mentored not only me and my siblings in our home but also a host of other aspiring and talented young musicians. I was also blessed to have a classroom in which to learn my trade that challenged me at every step of the way to be the best that I could possibly be and to strive for excellence. That classroom wasn't in some erudite Ivy League edifice on some distant college campus but in the Hampton home, as well as in the jazz clubs and fabled entertainment venues on Indiana Avenue. I learned so much at a young age jamming with the greatest musicians anyone could be fortunate enough to play with. Many of these musicians went on to international acclaim and recognition as jazz greats. I dare not mention any for fear I'd omit someone, and besides, the list would be long. They all were great!

Although I've won two Grammys, been honored by the National Endowment for the Arts with its highest honor (the Jazz Masters Award), been inducted into the Indianapolis Foundation Hall of Fame and performed all over the world, none of it would have been possible if not for my jazz education on Indiana Avenue.

As a youngster, as I jammed with these tremendous musicians, I sometimes would think that one day they'd all leave this earth and their history would be gone forever. In my heart of hearts, I always hoped that some way, somehow, this great history would be recorded. Now, with this book, written by David Williams, the lives and contributions of those great musicians of Indiana Avenue will live on! I'm so happy and thankful to David.

I endorse this book because I want to remember the great music educators and entertainers, like my parents, who labored long and hard and dedicated their lives so that all of my brothers and sisters in the entertainment community would be great people as well as outstanding musicians.

LOCKSLEY WELLINGTON "SLIDE" HAMPTON
November 7, 2013

Preface

"When you get to Naptown, the blues won't last very long, because they have their pleasure and they sure do carry on."
—lyrics to "Naptown Blues," composed by Leroy Carr, 1929

More than thirty years ago, I contemplated taking on the herculean task of writing the history of Indiana Avenue, and I struggled with my inner spirit, asking the question, "Why?" Indiana Avenue had long been a ghost of the past, owing to the expansion of Indiana University–Purdue University at Indianapolis (IUPUI). The Madam Walker Theatre Center had become a hollow shell with no resemblance to its glorious past, its edifice literally disintegrating. The nightclubs that once proudly offered the best of blues, jazz and rhythm-and-blues music had suddenly fallen silent.

Along with my personal doubt, I was constantly bombarded with a barrage of thought-provoking observations. People would challenge and criticize me, ask questions and make statements like, "Why are you writing about the Avenue? My daddy/mama, uncle/aunt always told me that all those Negroes did was to cut and shoot down there, and you heard ambulances all day and all night." I would hold my tongue and politely respond to these detractors, saying, "I was born and bred on the Avenue, and there was no more crime there than any other neighborhood in the city...the reason why ambulances were heard day and night was the fact that General Hospital's ambulance garage was a block away from the Avenue, and if there was an ambulance run to any part of the city, it had to pass by Indiana Avenue."

Suddenly, my inner being was producing a nostalgic collage of memories of my childhood being born and growing up at 810 Blake Street, apartment no. 77. I could see young me, snuggled in tight leggings and wooly hat with earmuffs, gloves and winter coat, with my beloved late sister, Betty Jean, being led by the hands of our grandmother Jessie Carson. We'd be walking toward Indiana Avenue and Blake Street, cattycorner from the Sunset Terrace Ballroom, to catch a streetcar (bus) to go downtown. As I thought about the collage more closely, I could see myself staring at a phalanx of black women waiting at the streetcar stop with scarves tied tightly around their necks, blowing in the December wind, lugging heavy brown shopping bags and chatting quietly among themselves. With the smoke of below-zero weather bellowing from their mouths, they still smiled and anticipated another workday. Inquisitively, I innocently looked up toward my grandmother and asked who the women were and where they were going.

Later, I learned that these women were residents of the Lockefield Gardens and surrounding neighborhoods who boarded the streetcars each morning to travel downtown to the Monument Circle. There they would transfer to other streetcars that would take them to Indianapolis neighborhoods like Golden Hills, Crow's Nest, Meridian Hills, Butler Tarkington, Irvington and all points in every direction. They would "work in private" or do "day work plus cab fare," which was a euphemism for being a maid. They would scrub floors, wash dishes, diaper babies, empty chamber pots and sometimes escape the clutches and sexual advances of flirtatious husbands.

On the other side of the street across from the Sunset Terrace Ballroom were the bootleg cab drivers. On many a below-zero morning, they would be huddled around a bonfire to keep warm in the parking lot next to Mr. Miller's Drug Store. They'd be waiting for a runner to exit the Chew 'N Chat Restaurant (where telephone calls were received to solicit a cab) and run across the street with a message to deliver to them so that they could pick up a fare.

They had to watch cautiously and be careful because city officials could arrest them for operating a cab without a license. But they knew that they had to "hustle" in order to feed a host of hungry mouths at home. From their accents and speech, I could discern that many were from the South and had little formal education, or "schooling," as they would explain. Many of these men were the fathers, uncles, brothers and cousins of Lockefield- and Indiana Avenue–area residents who, because of their limited education, were denied gainful employment at some of the better-paying places like the Eli Lilly Pharmaceutical Corporation, the Ford Motor Company or the Allison Transmission Corporation.

The historical events that occurred on Indiana Avenue during the past century were tightly intertwined with the entertainment industry in general and music in particular. In short, music was a metaphor for trials and tribulations that African Americans encountered. Contained within the lyrics of songs of many genres were the stories that reflected the history of Indiana Avenue. Interestingly, this phenomenon was evident not just here but also in other African American communities around the country.

In the early to mid-twentieth century in African American or ethnic communities across America, there were entertainment boulevards that exhibited robust commercial and artistic vitality that often defined these communities. Whether a record shop on the corner of 125th Street and Lenox Avenue in Harlem, a Creole restaurant in the French Quarter of New Orleans, a business on Springfield Avenue in Newark, a blues club on Beale Street in Memphis or the Texas Playhouse Bar in the Fillmore section of San Francisco, there has always been a heated debate as to whether the community defined the entertainment or the entertainment defined the community. Seemingly, music historians have often suggested a cause-and-effect scenario to answer this hypothetical question. The story of Indiana Avenue may present an alternative proposition.

The stretch of concrete and asphalt that winds serpent-like from Tenth Street to the north to Capitol Avenue to the south has been one of the keystones of Indiana history and the lifeblood of the African American community predating the Civil War. Since the days that the first former slaves stumbled exhaustedly into the city with barely shirts or dresses on their bodies or bread crumbs in their pockets in search of food and shelter, the definition of Indiana Avenue began to develop. Many of the slaves endured unspeakable cruelty and atrocities during slavery and were in search of an oasis of hope where they could quench their thirst for freedom.

It is my contention that the history that began with the catastrophic flood on White River in 1821 and ended with the demise of Indiana Avenue in the early 1970s defined Indiana Avenue and its entertainment empire. This symbiotic relationship between history, culture and entertainment has existed on the Avenue for many years. One could definitely correlate the murder of John Tucker on the corner of Michigan and Illinois Streets in 1845 with the guttural blues moaning of Yank Rachell singing a ballad of woe a century later. Or the connection between the announcement of the Emancipation Proclamation on a sweltering Tennessee slave plantation on January 1, 1863, and a ballad of good times and joy sung by the Hampton Sisters in 1953.

My passion for telling the stories of the musicians who performed on Indiana Avenue to appreciative, enthusiastic patrons is deep and one that I have held all of my adult life. The history is rich and broad. This particular book focuses on the extraordinary jazz musicians who performed on that fabled entertainment boulevard. Many of these musicians went on to become internationally famous, award-winning jazz masters. Wes Montgomery, J.J. Johnson, Slide Hampton, Leroy Vinnegar, David Baker, Monk Montgomery, Buddy Montgomery, Larry Ridley, Virgil Jones, Killer Ray Appleton, Phil Ranelin and James Spaulding are the names of a few.

The research and writing of this book has been a labor of love from the onset, and I am blessed to have had the opportunity to interact with so many people who were so extremely kind, generous and helpful. I must thank God, my creator, for giving me the strength to complete this project, and then my loving wife, Cynthia, and our children, David Jr. and Guenet Aster, for enduring years of discomfort as I labored in the vineyards late on countless nights with light bulbs glaring. I am deeply indebted to the staff of the Indiana Historical Society, the Indiana State Library, Dr. Pat Payne, the Indianapolis Public School Office of Multicultural Education and the Crispus Attucks Museum for providing me facilities in which to complete my research.

I am extremely grateful for the support that I received from Dr. Stanley Warren, Professor Emeritus of DePauw University; Wilma Gibbs-Moore, senior archivist for African American history, Indiana Historical Society; Nina Shirley-McCoy, Lockefield Gardens historian/artist; Susan Sutton, coordinator, visual reference services, Indiana Historical Society; Pamela Hurley-Shultz, computer specialist, Crispus Attucks Medical Magnet High School; Kisha Tandy, assistant curator of social history, Indiana State Museum; Winford Cork, jazz historian; and Janet Cheatham-Bell, publishing consultant. Also, I wish to thank my photographers, Duncan Schiedt, Larry Goshen, Mark Sheldon and Carl Black; my illustrator, Rodney Walker; and my videographer, Lewis Jones. Many thanks also for the financial contributions made by Fred Robinson, president, National Crispus Attucks Alumni Association; Tony Stuart, Stuart's Moving and Storage Company; and John Dumas Haamid, Lockefield Civic Organization.

There are a multitude of great individuals who gave of their precious time to ensure that this book would be completed, and if I omitted anyone, I am indeed truly sorry. The great folks include the late Mattie Louise Ferguson-Ballow, Carole Ferguson-Finnell, Dr. Richard Pierce, Kathleen Angelone, David Brent Johnson, Howard Daniel Pipes, John Dumas-Haamid, Rosalind

Dumas-Haamid, Eyassu Chernet, James Campbell, Harold Andrews, Freida Andrews, Waller Chapelle, Martha Chapelle, Thomas Ridley, Nancy Holliman-Johnson, Ruth Walker, Sheila Turner-Cooper, Winford Cork, Norma Martin-Cork, Ronald Cushenberry, A'Lelia Bundles, Henry Bundles, Nathan Wimberly, Marcia Wimberly, Paul Mullins, David Bodenhamer, Mari Evans, Olivia McGee-Lockhart, Aaron Hackney, Trevor Bacon Jr., Frazier King Jr., Fred Taylor, Marvin Chandler, Valerie Leggett-Davidson, Ellen Price-Sayles, Pamela R. Peters, Rozelle Boyd, Henry Woodruff, Dorothy Embry Whitfield, Louise Smith, Bill Hampton, William Pierson, Richard Pierson, Kenotis Foree, Ethel Milligan-Middlebrook, Larry Richard Shirley, Reginald DuValle, Mack Strong, Dennis Nichols, Charles Barker, Shirley Barker, Glenn White, Linda Bush, Darlene Parham, Margaret Mullins, Lorna Dawe, Nevoleane Ridley, Betty Fowlkes-Norfleet, Audrey Buford-Taylor, Henry Woods Jr., Pearl Foster, Karen Taborn, John Gipson, Stephen Dale, Edith Glover, John Montgomery, Bill Hampton, Dona Stokes-Lucas, Bill Steiner, Chuck Workman, Edith Fitzhugh, Ellen Perkins-Strickling, Anna Coleman, Mary Ruth Bernard-Black, Godfrey Muhammad, Ann Sutter, Olivia McGee-Lockhart, Lexie Webster and Woodie Carpenter.

In essence, I wrote this book as a tribute to the musicians whose lives and careers are chronicled here. It's a way to tell the stories of those who went on to great acclaim and achievement, as well as to acknowledge those jazz masters whose names are largely unknown. Equally, this book is dedicated to the hardworking and fun-loving patrons who crowded the many clubs and entertainment venues along the Avenue and heard music composed and performed by those innovative, dedicated, extraordinarily gifted and creative musicians of Indiana Avenue.

There are many stories and events that occurred on the Avenue, and it is this author's hope that the interaction between history, culture and entertainment on Indiana Avenue can be examined and appreciated.

Chapter 1

Early Indianapolis

Indiana Avenue—"Street of Dreams," "Majestic Boulevard," "Entertainment Mecca of the Midwest." All of these and many more superlatives described the ribbon of concrete and asphalt that stretched from City Hospital and Tenth Street on the north to Ohio Street and downtown on the south. It was the heart and soul of the African American community. Its identity became so powerfully influential and all-encompassing that it was difficult to determine where its personality began and that of the African American community ended. Or perhaps they were the same—two great identities fused into one. Down this mesmerizing stretch of concrete and humanity, people could behold the sights, sounds, smells, music and people that gave Indiana Avenue its upbeat, creative character.

In the Avenue's heyday, a person might see an advertisement poster nailed to a telephone pole at Blake Street and Indiana Avenue, directly across from Denver Ferguson's Sunset Terrace Ballroom. Heralding a little-known piano player and vocalist originally from Montgomery, Alabama, but raised in Chicago, the poster would scream, "Nat King Cole Trio at the Sunset Terrace Tonight." There might be a billboard in the front of the P&P Club announcing the "Sassy and Classy Divine One," Sarah Vaughan and Her Orchestra, or a 1930s vintage advertisement truck slowly creeping down the Avenue with a gigantic public announcement system mounted on top broadcasting to all that after a two-year absence, the Fantabulous Mr. Billy Eckstein would return to Sea Ferguson's Cotton Club. Many of the greatest entertainers in the world performed on the Avenue. It would be accurate to say that there was a hot and heavy love affair between these towering entertainers and the patrons they serenaded.

In addition to the immortals of the stage, screen and recording studios like Duke Ellington, Count Basie, Cab Calloway, Lionel Hampton, Lucky Millinder, Charlie Parker and Miles Davis, there were others. There were many local greats and near-greats who were overshadowed by their out-of-town contemporaries. Their only fault was that locals saw these folks every day and somehow took their greatness for granted. Most of them could not afford to take the chance of hitting the road in the quest for fame and fortune because they had many responsibilities that prohibited them from undertaking out-of-town travel; this factor obviously limited their regional and national exposure. They were great entertainers, without a doubt— Indianapolis's best-kept secret.

On January 1, 1863, when President Abraham Lincoln signed the Emancipation Proclamation, it signaled the termination of the cruel and inhumane system of slavery in the Confederate States of America. Many former slaves, determined to carve out a more palatable existence, headed north or, in their folk vernacular, "up south." On foot, blacks began a trek to a promised land where they hoped to live in harmony with other human beings and improve their lots in life. From numerous points behind the cotton curtain, black folks were on the move. Many had received information by word of mouth that the quality of life would be much better up south.

One could visualize a lonely ex-slave traveling the winding dusty roads northward to Indianapolis, mindful of the fact that only a short while prior, this journey would have been highlighted by a pack of slave owner's snarling, yelping bloodhounds nipping at his heels and trailing him in hot pursuit. With the idea of freedom on his mind and the anticipation of a new beginning in the North, the ex-slave may have entertained visions of a quiet and peaceful life up south devoid of the trials and tribulations that he had previously endured down south. He may have joyfully contemplated cities such as Evansville, Indianapolis, Chicago or Detroit as being possible destinations where he could enjoy the fruits of his newfound freedom. Unfortunately, what this black refugee would soon realize was that the same degree of poverty, oppression and hard times from which he had escaped in the South was waiting up the road and welcoming him with open arms as he entered a new Promised Land: Indiana.

Arriving in Indianapolis after the Emancipation Proclamation, blacks discovered that there was a welcoming community of African Americans situated near the center of the city along the White River. This community—which would later be referred to as Bucktown, Sleigho or Colored Town—provided the refugees with some semblance of normalcy and helped them settle into a new living situation. Weary travelers would rejoice over meeting relatives and friends whom they had assumed they would never see again after fleeing the South. Indeed, this area was a refuge where all could try to forget the pain of their slavery past and anticipate a new beginning in the North.

As curious ex-slaves trickled into the city of Indianapolis, they were greeted with sights reminiscent of their native South. Rickety shacks, dilapidated shanties and other apparent shelters dotted the banks of the White River as swirls of white smoke belched from rustic chimneys, signaling a welcome to the new inhabitants. Many of the blacks who arrived brought little more than the clothes on their backs. However, in spite of their lack of tangible possessions, they brought an enormous determination to repair family structures and chart a new course. Many families were fractured during slavery when slave owners sold family members to other plantations.

These newcomers brought folklore and tall tales that they were eager to share with their northern neighbors, as well as anyone else who might listen. They brought a desire to amuse them and relive the few fond memories they cherished of the South. Perhaps it was the cheerful memory of a slave wedding, when bride and groom would jump over a broom indicating the union of two souls, or the birth of a baby, when at midnight with the stars ablaze its tiny body was lifted toward heaven by strong, callused black hands and the words declared, "Behold the only thing greater than yourself."

It is very likely that some of the musically gifted new inhabitants may have entertained their homesick neighbors by playing ditties of the South. Field and spiritual songs called holler chants gave many of the new inhabitants a connection with their antebellum past. Entertainers of all genres of music performed in small establishments along the trails surrounding White River to the delight of their neighbors. Thus, the seeds were sown that would later blossom into the beautiful flower named Indiana Avenue, an entertainment empire.

In 1899, Scott Joplin, the Texas-born composer considered to be the "Father of Ragtime Music," wrote the "Maple Leaf Rag," which became the greatest piano rag of all times. After its release, ragtime music swept the country and immediately had a major impact on Indiana Avenue and surrounding neighborhoods. Even two wealthy, German-American young ladies, May Aufderheide and Julia Niebergall, were bitten by the ragtime bug, writing the "Dusty Rag" and the "Horseshoe Rag," respectively.

Seemingly by cultural diffusion, the impact of Joplin's music slowly seeped into the nightclubs and juke joints along Indiana Avenue and ignited the entertainment explosion. In 1977, the movie *The Sting* (which was the winner of seven Academy Awards, including Best Picture) featured excerpts from his composition "The Entertainer" on its soundtrack and sparked a nationwide revival of Joplin's ragtime music.

The *Freeman* newspaper, a weekly owned by businessman George Knox, covered the Joplin ragtime explosion and served as the town crier for entertainment events on Indiana Avenue. It contained an entire page dedicated to local, regional and national entertainment. In the majority of the editions, there were advertisements from businesses around the country seeking "colored" singers and dancers to perform in minstrel and coon shows that would ultimately tour the nation. Several of these shows appeared at the Park Theatre, the English Opera House and Tim Owlsley's New Crown Garden. Many of the minstrel acts that appeared on the Avenue consisted of two principal performers, like Cole & Johnson or Tim & Gertie.

Interestingly, Timothy and Gertrude Moore of Rock Island, Illinois, had an extremely popular revue that played to standing room–only audiences along the Avenue. Decades later, Tim Moore would make television history by being the principal actor in a controversial 1950s black situation comedy entitled *Amos 'n' Andy*. His character was the conniving, scheming George "Kingfish" Stevens, who would always pull shenanigans on the dimwitted, gullible Andrew J. Brown. Kingfish was married to the domineering, dictatorial, screechy-voiced Sapphire, whose persona became a stereotypical model of black women of this period. Many African American civil rights organizations, including the National Association for the Advancement of Colored People (NAACP), protested this as the only television portrayal of the African American family. The program was removed from the television lineup.

Russell Smith, an accomplished black pianist, often appeared in the *Freeman* newspaper and received rave reviews with the publishing of the "Princess Rag" in 1907 and the "Microbe Rag" and "Demon Rag" in 1911. The following year, he wrote the music and lyrics, with T.L. Cornwell and J. Homer Tutt, for the hilarious blockbuster musical comedy *The Dark Town Politician*. It was highly praised in the local newspapers and successfully launched Russell Smith's career. It is likely that the saloons, barrelhouses and juke joints that dotted Indiana Avenue had the ragtime sounds of Russell Smith floating harmoniously in the air. One can almost imagine seeing Smith, with a big cigar plugged into his mouth, sitting at the piano and belting out an original ragtime tune to the delight of drinking and frolicking customers.

Many black musicians who polished their craft on the Avenue earned their livelihood by performing for aristocratic white patrons in the more affluent neighborhoods of Indianapolis. It is likely that some of these aristocrats may have ventured to Indiana Avenue to escape the boredom of their routine existence. Perhaps they desired to enjoy the full atmospheric impact of the colorful people and incredible music that became synonymous with the Avenue. When black musicians and entertainers performed at some white venues away from the Avenue, they regretfully realized that they had to decrease the tempo of some songs in order to satisfy the musical taste of their white patrons. Submitting to the patrons' demands, blacks also had to include various genres of European music in their repertoire, such as waltzes, mazurkas, schottisches and novelty two-steps, as well as the grand march, which was the highlight of the evening.

As the melodic sounds of ragtime piano riffs continued to reverberate inside taverns, saloons and juke joints along Indiana Avenue and float out the doors into the nighttime breeze, the smell of human sweat, mixed with alcohol and cigar smoke, accentuated the merriment that was experienced by all who had entered these venues. Entertainment was king, and word spread quickly throughout the city that if one wanted to have an uproariously great time, one would have to venture on to Indiana Avenue after dark. Many entertainers of all genres, wanting to gain a foothold in this fledgling entertainment industry, came from near and far to the Avenue in the hope of finding their proverbial pot of gold at the end of the rainbow.

One such musician was Ben Holliman, who was born on May 28, 1886, in Henderson, Texas. Having recently graduated from high school, young Ben followed his older brother, James, who had opened a restaurant on Indiana Avenue, and began to help him run the business. After Ben had worked in many facets of the restaurant business, the daily chores became monotonous, and he became disillusioned. But after deep meditation and soul searching, he replaced the sounds of clanking pots and pans in the kitchen and the screeching sounds of chairs sliding under tables with the sounds of a soulfully sweet saxophone solo and a machine gun–timed drumroll. He met and associated himself with established Indiana Avenue musicians such as Reginald DuValle Sr., Tedd Cable, Charlie Carr, Charlie Brown and Frank Brown. He taught himself to play the saxophone, guitar, ukulele, banjo and mandolin and then performed with various musical groups on Indiana Avenue.

Word of Holliman's musical genius became common knowledge on the Avenue, and many enterprising, determined bandleaders made a beeline to his door in order to acquire his services. Broadway songwriters and composers Noble Sissle and Eubie Blake, who frequently traveled from New York to Indianapolis scouting new talent, quickly contacted young Holliman and took him under their wings. Holliman became a prominent member of the electrifying Reginald DuValle and His Blackbyrds Orchestra and toured throughout the region, performing at luxurious white nightclubs and private venues. Also, young Holliman tested his songwriting skills and composed a ragtime hit entitled "The Jungle Society Ball."

A significant influence on the artistic development of Ben Holliman was the great songwriter, composer and pianist Russell Smith. William Russell Smith was born in June 1890 to Frances Smith in Versailles, Kentucky. Raised and educated in Indianapolis, Smith is reported to have been the first African American to conduct an orchestra in Indianapolis's downtown entertainment district. In 1911, as a pianist and vocalist, he established a residency at the Severin Hotel with notable sidemen Reginald DuValle, Noble Sissle and Eubie Blake. In the 1920s, Smith performed as a comedian in the New York Broadway productions of *Shuffle Along* and *Chocolate Dandies*. A decade later, he became the arranger for the W.C. Handy Music Publishing Company in New York.

Russell Smith, a musician who mentored many of the early Indiana Avenue entertainers, including the father of Nancy Holliman-Johnson. *Courtesy of Duncan Schiedt.*

Nancy Holliman-Johnson, Ben Holliman's daughter, related a very interesting as well as comical story relative to her father's relationship to Smith. She said that Smith was very fond of imbibing alcoholic spirits and would often visit their home to perform on the grand piano. On many occasions, Smith would have stopped by the local tavern for a taste or two or three, and by the time he arrived at the Holliman house, he would be quite affected by those alcoholic spirits. He quietly tapped on the front door to announce his arrival and then entered with a wobbly-legged gait, pounced on the piano bench and played a magnificent ragtime roll as he scooted down the bench in unison with the music. After reaching the end of the bench, he would fall on the floor and then regain his footing and dust himself off, only to fall again. The Holliman girls, both Nancy and Louise, would giggle with excitement at the hilarious spectacle that Smith presented.

There was another interesting personality who often visited the Holliman home on the weekends and who many years later gained international fame and fortune in the world of music. Young Hoagy Carmichael, then a student at Indiana University, roamed the clubs along Indiana Avenue listening to the music of Reginald DuValle, Louie Jordan and Albert "Fats" Johnson, picking up musical points that he would later incorporate into his compositions. He would visit the Holliman home as well as the DuValles' (more about this later) to discuss the latest trends in music that he had heard in the clubs. Carmichael was also interested in receiving instruction on the Indiana Avenue school of thought relative to performing popular music, composing sensational tunes and playing notes that were contrary to the musical theories of collegiate instruction. On many quiet evenings, Carmichael would dine at the Holliman home and then engage Ben Holliman on aspects of music theory. According to Nancy Holliman-Johnson, young Carmichael would arrive at the front door with his signature hat cocked askew on his head and with a brilliant, welcoming smile. He would enter their home and go directly to the living room, where there was a large, oak bedroom dresser with an oval-shaped mirror in the center and two drawer compartments on either side. Carmichael would sit between the drawer compartments with his back to the mirror and jokingly proclaim himself "Chief of the Bungleloos." This line was taken from Ben Holliman's song "Jungle Society Ball." The Holliman family was always amused at Carmichael's penchant for comedy and his happy spirit.

Chapter 2

The Roarin' Twenties

Noble Sissle was born on July 10, 1889, in Indianapolis in a large A-frame wooden house located on Columbia Avenue on the city's east side. That house is now the annex for St. John African Methodist Episcopal (AME) Church at 1669 Columbia Avenue. His father was a public school teacher for several years and then changed careers and became a minister. His mother was also a schoolteacher. She had taught in school systems in Ohio and Kentucky, where she met and married her husband in 1888. At a time when African Americans were slowly drifting into town, living in dilapidated shacks near White River and surviving by their wits, the Sissle family was comparatively living in the lap of luxury. Many of their neighbors were members of Indianapolis's black aristocracy, composed of doctors, lawyers and merchants.

In 1906, Reverend Sissle was called to lead the Cory Methodist Episcopal Church in Cleveland, Ohio. In Cleveland, Noble attended and graduated from Central High School, where he was a president of the Glee Club and class vocalist. He also sang in the choir in his father's church. Seeds were silently being sown for vaudeville that would germinate many years later. Unexpectedly, his father fell ill and died in 1913, whereupon the grief-stricken family returned to Indianapolis to be closer to family members and friends.

Back in Indianapolis, Sissle quickly reestablished his musical roots and organized his own orchestra, which he led at the all-white Severin Hotel located downtown. He left for Baltimore in 1915 and met Eubie

Blake there. They were band members of Joe Porter's Serenaders. Sissle teamed up with Blake and traveled to New York City, where they wrote and produced the first black Broadway smash sensation, *Shuffle Along*. After experiencing success and national acclaim in New York, Sissle and Blake would frequently return to Indianapolis to scout new talent.

Another individual and contemporary of Sissle's who had a considerable impact on the popularity of music and entertainment on Indiana Avenue was Reginald Alfred DuValle. Born on October 22, 1893, in Indianapolis to Emma

Noble Sissle wrote the Butler University fight song, teamed up with Eubie Blake and produced musicals on Broadway.

McCann DuValle and Alfred DuValle, he graduated from Shortridge High School in 1911, long before Indianapolis high schools were segregated. While at Shortridge, he developed a profound interest in music and would organize musical groups to provide entertainment for school dances and other events. After graduation, young DuValle landed an enviable spot as pianist in one of the hottest groups on or off the Avenue, the Russell Smith Orchestra. He performed with these gentlemen for a few years until he gained enough experience to blaze his own trail.

From his performance in the Russell Smith Orchestra, news of DuValle's musical brilliance circulated throughout the region, and he began to receive more financially lucrative engagements from all corners of the state. Perhaps the crowning achievement of his musical accomplishments was that his orchestra, Reginald DuValle's Blackbyrds, opened the world-famous (and now national historic landmark) Walker Building on December 26, 1927. In addition to his immense popularity on the Avenue, DuValle was contracted

Reginald DuValle Sr. fronted an orchestra that opened the Walker Theatre in 1927 and mentored a young Hoagy Carmichael. *Courtesy of Indiana Historical Society.*

by local radio station WKBF to perform on the accordion and piano as the Rhythm King.

In addition to being an eminent musical personality on the Avenue, DuValle mentored many up-and-coming music students who would venture on to the Avenue to polish their skills and techniques while learning an entirely different and improvisational approach to music. One such student he mentored was Hoagy Carmichael. While attending Indiana University, young Carmichael would board a train on Fridays after class and head for Indianapolis. Once in Indianapolis, he went directly to 1202 Harlan Street on the city's south side, where he received instruction at the knee of DuValle. Carmichael remembered in his book *The Star Dust Road,* "My mother tried to teach me to play piano, but I was just twelve years old and it was all by ear and I don't think, I remembered a thing about it later, if it hadn't been for a great black piano player named Reggie DuValle. He showed me the art of improvising, using the third and sixth of the chord as a basis for arpeggios."

DuValle's young son, Reginald Jr., who was a toddler at the time, recalled, "In our home, we seldom had any white people, so he kind of stood out, if you know what I mean." Reginald Jr. also related a story that took place during the Great Depression in which his father, desperate for money to feed his family, sold sheet music to white bandleader Charlie Davis for five dollars. He later discovered that the title of one of his songs had been changed to "Copenhagen," which became one of the most popular tunes of this period.

The trombonist in Reginald DuValle's Blackbyrds that opened the Walker Building was Wheeler Morin. Morin was born to Fred and Sarah Morin in 1910 in Muncie, Indiana. Early in his professional career,

Hoagy Carmichael frequented Indiana Avenue and sharpened his musical skills. He became an internationally known songwriter.

he adopted the stage name "Doc Wheeler" and left Indianapolis for the bright lights of New York City. There, he joined the Sunset Royals Orchestra, which was previously known as the Florida Collegiates and later became Doc Wheeler and His Sunset Orchestra. Doc Wheeler was the arranger on the Ink Spots' 1939 blockbuster hit "If I Didn't Care."

Doc Wheeler and His Sunset Orchestra obtained an RCA contract and recorded the song "Who Threw the Whisky in the Well?" which was a popular tune during the 1940s. The group was composed of several musicians who would later distinguish themselves in the orchestras of Duke Ellington and Count Basie. They performed at Harlem's famed Savoy Room, the Cotton Club and the Apollo Theater. In 1944, Doc Wheeler married former Cotton Club showgirl Julia Noisette and began a radio broadcasting career spinning gospel tunes at WWRL radio station in Woodside, Long Island.

Doc Wheeler played in various family bands on Indiana Avenue. *Courtesy of Duncan Schiedt.*

Beryl William Steiner was another of the musicians who played for DuValle. Steiner was born in Indianapolis on July 7, 1915. His parents were William "Bud" Steiner and Leona Marie Bernadette Ashley Steiner. Beryl's earliest introduction to music was in 1924, when he took saxophone lessons from Louis Lorenz, a musician in the brass section of the Indianapolis Symphony Orchestra. In 1928, Steiner entered Crispus Attucks High School and joined the marching band under the direction of music educator Harold Brown. That same year, bandleader DuValle Sr. was in desperate need of musicians who could read music—several of his musicians were excellent artists but could not read music. This required DuValle to spend additional time teaching them new music scores. DuValle contacted Harold Brown to secure a saxophonist for his aggregation. Brown recommended Steiner, who was his most outstanding student and a star saxophonist. Steiner auditioned for DuValle and was so impressive that DuValle hired him on the spot. His first gig with the DuValle orchestra was in 1929 at the Indianapolis Athletic Club at 350 North Meridian Street. Later, Steiner performed with the Brown Buddies, a group of Crispus Attucks High School musicians named in honor of their music teacher, Harold Brown. They performed in many of the jazz venues along Indiana Avenue but primarily at Sea Ferguson's Cotton Club.

During the Great Depression, the music scene in Indianapolis took a turn for the worse as patrons lost homes and jobs and entertainment venues closed on the Avenue. The economic picture in America was very gloomy, and citizens struggled just to make ends meet. Steiner remembered, "Poor folks didn't go to nightclubs in those days. We'd earn a dollar a night wages plus tips. Well, some nights they'd [patrons] walk up, put a dollar or five dollars in the kitty [collection jar] and we'd go divide the kitty and go home with one to twenty-five dollars per man. Sure got my father irritated with me 'cause he only made seven dollars per week. During the Depression, good money was twenty-five cents a night plus tips, and big bucks were two dollars a night." Later, Steiner performed with the Wisdom Brothers' (Fred and Henry) Band at Sea Ferguson's Cotton Club located at 242 West Vermont Street.

In the mid-1930s, Steiner joined Chick Carter's band in Columbus, Ohio, then went farther east and joined the Jimmy Watkins Band, and both bands performed regionally on the Chitlin' Circuit and had limited national exposure. The Chitlin' Circuit was a network of entertainment venues operated exclusively for African American audiences because segregationist policy dictated the separation of the races. He also performed with comedians Butterbeans & Suzy and Sunshine Sammy (Ernie Morrison) from the *Our Gang* comedy short film series produced by Hal Roach during the 1920s.

While Steiner performed with the Jimmy Watkins Band, blues singer and motion picture star Ethel Waters bought his contract. For two years, he played road shows with her band in the late 1930s. Waters took the band to New York to seek "fame and fortune," and Steiner promptly got laid off with what he swore was just a nickel in his pocket. Later, he teamed with fellow alto saxophonist Don Byas, who had earlier won national acclaim performing with the Lionel Hampton Orchestra at the Paradise Club in Los Angeles. Waters called Steiner back to the band in time to record her first album, *Jeepers Creepers*, with music by Harry Warren and lyrics by Johnny Mercer, for Radio Corporation of America (RCA) on November 9, 1938.

In 1940, Steiner returned to Indianapolis, tired of the hustle and bustle of New York and the toll it had taken on him. He was thirty-five years old and weighed 145 pounds. "I was so skinny when I held my hand up sideways, I could hide. With no family, no bank account, no nothing else, I told Byas he could stay if he wanted to, but I was going home and after that I wasn't ever goin' no further than I have to." In Indianapolis, Steiner hooked up with the Lucky Millinder Orchestra and joined fellow Indianapolis resident and vocalist Trevor Bacon, who later recorded "When the Lights Go On Again All Over the World," which reached the no. 1 spot on the rhythm-and-blues chart in 1942.

Steiner's relationship with the domineering, dictatorial and overbearing Millinder proved to be contentious and problematic, with a series of troubling episodes. Millinder fired Steiner five times and rehired him four times, but after the fifth firing, Steiner had enough and said, "I wouldn't go back, I just quit." In the June 1, 1940 edition of the *Indianapolis Recorder*, Steiner is reported to have returned to Indianapolis after touring with Lucky Millinder, Ethel Waters and pianist/bandleader Edgar Hayes. It further reported that he performed a saxophone solo at a June recital by students of the Cosmopolitan School of Music and Fine Arts located at 2602 Northwestern Avenue, sponsored by Phillips Temple Colored Methodist Episcopal (CME) Church located at 1226 West Street.

Steiner attended Purdue University and graduated from Butler University and had a thirty-three-year career with Citizens Gas and Coke Utility Company. Steiner lamented the entertainment scene on Indiana Avenue, saying, "The market for good music collapsed. It wasn't the market's place to provide a continuous stage for jazz—the market was out for the dollar… they pay $200 to some disc jockey to stand up and make spicy commentary and not contribute a thing. If you're lucky, you can still catch some of the lake resort nightclubs in northern Indiana or in Michigan or Wisconsin." In the following decades, from time to time, Steiner gigged on the Avenue with various groups such as the Dudley Storms, Eldridge Morrison, Jimmy Coe and Larry Liggett big bands and with the Bob Womack and Willis Kirk small ensembles at many of the jazz venues that lined Indiana Avenue. Beryl William Steiner died on November 28, 1983, in Indianapolis.

Against this background of sensational news stories in black America, the struggle for daily existence continued on Indiana Avenue. Barrelhouses, saloons and juke joints continued to open, and a new music genre called the blues invaded the entertainment scene. In early 1920, Sophie Tucker, the world-famous Jewish entertainer who sang burlesque and vaudevillian tunes in blackface, became ill and missed a blues recording date. Perry Bradford, the songwriter, convinced the Okeh record company to instead record African American Mamie Smith, a singer-dancer. As the saying goes, the rest is history. The record "Crazy Blues" sold ten thousand recordings during the first week and seventy-five thousand recordings within a month, totals that were barely comprehendible during this period. Many black female singers took note of Smith's commercial triumph and began flocking to recording studios around the country in an attempt to duplicate her feat.

The blues, which some call the "Father of Jazz," made its initial introduction on Indiana Avenue with blues warblers Ida Cox and Edmonia Henderson, who performed at the Washington Theatre in the early 1920s. A decade later, Leroy Carr and Francis "Scrapper" Blackwell continued to showcase the genre at many juke joints and holes in the wall along the entertainment strip. Throughout the 1940s, "Champion Jack" Dupree was the preeminent "honker and shouter" and packed them in nightly at Sea Ferguson's Cotton Club.

Ida Cox began her musical career as a singer in church choirs in her native Georgia. She ran away from home as a teenager and performed in tent and minstrel shows throughout the Midwest. Later, she sang with nationally known entertainment greats such as Jelly Roll Morton and King Oliver. In the 1920s, Cox appeared on many occasions to packed houses at the Washington Theatre, located at 521 Indiana Avenue. Her signature songs that nightly brought down the house included "Blues Ain't Nothin' But" and "Booze Crazy Man Blues."

At the dawn of the twentieth century in Indianapolis, a system of social stratification developed that was based on education, skin color, hair texture, years removed from slavery and proper European-like comportment. There were pretentious, high society–minded African Americans who did not want to be associated with recently migrated ex-slaves from the South, but this was an insignificant number. There were lighter-complexioned African Americans who lived on the fringes of society in poverty along with their darker-complexioned counterparts, and Henderson's song "Brown-Skin

Man" exploited this color difference. The song pitted darker-skinned African Americans against lighter-complexioned African Americans. Some of the lyrics delivered a comparative study of the alleged virtues and vices of "high yellow" and brown men: "a high yellow [man] will throw you and that ain't all / every night they usually home another mule in your stall / a brown skin man will love you, / will surely treat you right, / stay at home and do his work both day and night… / a brown skin man is alright, / a yellow man get twenty-five, he slowly draws up like rice." Indeed, Edmonia Henderson was a magnificent talent albeit a controversial figure.

Henderson was a chubby-cheeked, rotund blues diva who arrived on the Avenue in the early 1920s and immediately electrified the blues aficionados with her gutsy barrelhouse notes and powerful vocal delivery. A news release in one of the trade journals read, "Edmonia is an old-time stage favorite, who has been in big-time vaudeville for years. She recently won the Paramount Blues Singer Contest. Henderson leaped into fame with her famous song 'Brown-Skin Man'—a song that will never grow old, and is selling faster every month. Edmonia has an exclusive, clever, melodious way of warbling her Blues—the kind that will make you forget work and trouble and will make you want to listen to more. Put your money on Edmonia. You will never be sorry." Henderson was certainly an accomplished blues singer, but "Brown-Skin Man" ignited a controversy that had long been simmering beneath the surface in the black community.

A decade after rhythm and blues, the offspring of doo wop, electrified Indiana Avenue, a soft-spoken, willowy man with a deep southern accent strolled on to the Avenue with a mandolin tucked under his arm. Heretofore, both music historians and blues purists had not considered the mandolin to be a bona fide blues instrument but rather regarded it as a novelty instrument almost akin to a toy. When James Rachell arrived in town, he forever changed all those preconceived ideas and artistic prejudices.

James "Yank" Rachell was born to George Rachell and Lula Taylor Rachell on March 16, 1910, on a small farm on the outskirts of Brownsville, Tennessee. As a farm boy whose daily chores included milking cows, shucking corn and picking and chopping cotton, as well as doing small chores around the house, he had little time for entertainment. However, Rachell was introduced to the world of music one day while walking down a dusty Tennessee road. Legend has it that at the tender age of eight, Rachell's mother gave him a pig with the strict instructions that he was to raise the animal until it could be slaughtered in the fall. One day while walking down the road, he saw a neighbor who was playing a mandolin on his front porch, and Yank was fascinated by the beautiful sound that resonated from the box. Excitedly, he asked the man how much money he wanted for his mandolin, and the man responded, "Five dollars." Rachell reached into his dusty pocket and couldn't find a penny, so he offered the man a deal. He told the man that he would return home and fetch his prize pig and trade it for the mandolin. The man agreed. Later, back at home, his mother was desperately searching around the farm and deep into the thickets looking for the pig. She asked him if he knew where the pig was. "No, ma'am," he innocently replied. Finally, after an intensive interrogation, Rachell broke down, told the truth and admitted that he had traded the pig for his newly acquired mandolin. Since he finally told the truth, his mother did not whip him but instead angrily asserted, "Come next fall, when we all eatin' pork, you can eat that mandolin!"

Shortly thereafter, Rachell began to fiddle around with the mandolin, devising a system to teach himself to play. Soon he was introduced to a local musician named "Hambone" Willie Newbern, who was proficient on the mandolin. Newbern taught Rachell basic chords and fingering techniques, and Rachell began to polish the rough edges of his musical skills. Soon, the two were performing at juke joints, fish fries and house parties around Brownsville and became very popular entertainers.

At one of these events, Rachell met "Sleepy John" Estes and Hammie Nixon. According to Rachell, "Me and singer and guitarist Sleepy John were stickin' around together and then picked up harmonica player Hammie and taught him how to play." The trio performed as a jug band, with homemade instruments like washtubs, spoons and kazoos, throughout Tennessee and adjoining states for both black and white audiences. He recalled that when they performed for white farmers and earned four dollars per night, it was considered "good money" during the 1920s. In the mid-1920s, the trio relocated to Memphis, Tennessee, where they could earn more money, and their popularity skyrocketed. With the departure of Hammie Nixon, they acquired pianist Jab Jones and formed the Three J's Jug Band, which became a popular attraction in clubs on Beale Street during the Memphis jug band craze.

Rachell and his group recorded ten songs, but the recording industry was one of the many casualties of the Great Depression. Dejectedly, Rachell returned to Brownsville and began to farm; later, he got a job on the Louisville & Nashville (L&N) Railroad. He married, started a family and would occasionally play at fish fries and house parties on the weekends. He relocated to St. Louis, and then in 1958, he came to Indianapolis with his ailing wife and family. His wife died three years later. In 1962, while Rachell was living in Indianapolis, he located his old buddy "Sleepy John" Estes living quietly back in Brownsville. The two of them found Hammie Nixon, and the trio began performing together again at coffee houses, concerts and festivals throughout the United States and Europe. They were immensely popular on college campuses. In the 1990s, Rachell was rediscovered again and performed nightly before adoring blues fans at an Indianapolis blues club called the Slippery Noodle. He recorded several CDs and really basked in the attention and glory that his newfound celebrity provided him. Yank Rachell made his final curtain call on April 9, 1997.

While James "Yank" Rachell was strumming his mandolin to the delight of his neighbors in the backwoods of west Tennessee, Leroy Jennings picked up a guitar and began to play for his family members and friends on Indiana Avenue. William Leroy Jennings was born to Albert Jennings Jr. and Garnet Jennings on September 12, 1919, in Indianapolis. With his guitar, he was a permanent entertainment fixture in many of the jazz venues on Indiana Avenue. In the 1930s, he joined his brother, guitarist Al Jennings, and they performed on radio station WLW in Cincinnati. They continued to perform together until World War I, when they entered the United States Armed Forces. At the conclusion of the war, he led his own combo in St. Louis and later joined the Louis Jordan Tympany Five band. He remained with the Jordan aggregation for three years, and then he freelanced and performed with various groups, including with baritone saxophonist Leo Parker. He also recorded with bandleader Bill Doggett, organist "Brother Jack" McDuff and the Willis Jackson Quintet. He was inspired by guitarist Les Paul, whom he admired for his "multiple techniques and beat." Jennings died on December 4, 1978.

Chapter 3

Dawn of the Walker Theatre

Another blues musician and contemporary of Yank Rachell's was Arthur "Montana" Taylor, who frequented the barrelhouses and saloons on Indiana Avenue listening to the various musicians and entertainers and being greatly affected by them. Early influences on his musical development included Tom and Phil Harding, two brothers "who could really play the blues," according to Taylor. Also, there were two other Indiana Avenue musical personalities, "Slick" Helms and Jimmy Collins, who impressed him immensely.

Taylor was born to Archibald and Olivia Taylor in 1903 in Butte, Montana, where his father owned and operated a saloon. In 1910, his family relocated to Chicago, Illinois, and then to Indianapolis, Indiana. During his middle teen years, he began to practice the piano, perhaps recalling his father's earlier venture in Montana. In 1923, one of Taylor's first professional gigs was playing in a dilapidated structure located in the most depressed and dangerous area of Indiana Avenue, appropriately called Rag Alley. The barrelhouse called the Hole in the Wall was owned by local businessman Henry "Goosie" Lee. Legend has it that the notorious Indiana gangster John Dillinger entered this establishment one night to be entertained and purchase a drink but only stayed a few minutes after surveying the premises and seeing the dangerous characters in attendance. It was reported that Taylor earned only a few dollars per night performing for the rowdy, dangerous customers who frequented this joint. Montana Taylor died in 1954.

It is interesting to note that ragtime and blues music and minstrel and vaudevillian shows were not the only entertainment genres that attracted

Arthur "Montana" Taylor played in juke joints on Indiana Avenue and performed for John Dillinger. *Courtesy of Cleveland Public Library.*

Fleet of busy taxicabs parked in front of the Walker Theatre waiting for matinee patrons to exit, circa 1940. *Courtesy of Tony Stuart.*

patrons to Indiana Avenue. Spiritual music was also very popular, and in a sense, it neutralized the secular atmosphere of the Avenue. Bethel African Methodist Episcopal (AME) Church, located on Vermont Street just a stone's throw from the Avenue, contributed to the different forms of music that gave the Avenue its unique character. Floating from its multicolored, ornate stained-glass windows were beautiful sounds that would blend with the more secular musical genres and give the Avenue a multifaceted artistic appeal. Spiritual groups from near and far would perform at the church, and the melodious sounds emanating from this edifice were beautiful to hear. One such group was the Foster Hall Quartet.

In the mid- to late 1920s, there was a musical group sponsored by the Senate Avenue YMCA, also in proximity to Indiana Avenue, called the Colored YMCA Quartet. This group specialized in spiritual songs and was very popular in the religious community. Josiah Kirby Lilly Jr.—businessman, philanthropist, community leader and collector of fine art—was the grandson of Colonel Eli Lilly, a Civil War veteran who in 1876 founded the pharmaceutical giant that bears his name. Josiah Lilly came to the weekly forums at the YMCA called Monster Meetings. Here, many of the finest African American scholars, educators and business leaders delivered lectures

The Foster Hall Quartet, a spiritual quintet employed by the millionaire grandson of Colonel Eli Lily, changed its repertoire to Stephen Foster songs.

to the community on social, political and economic issues. Lilly attended these forums to keep abreast of local, national and international issues and to keep his finger on the pulse of the Indianapolis African American community. Being an avid collector of fine art, he developed an insatiable thirst for the music and artifacts of songwriter Stephen Foster. He found great delight in every song that Foster penned and was determined to glorify Foster's legend by preserving his music and presenting it to the fine arts community on a continual basis. He took the talented Colored YMCA Quartet under his wing and renamed it the Foster Hall Quartet in honor of Stephen Foster.

The members of the Foster Hall Quartet were George Marion Robinson, Wallace Wolfolk, Clarence Hicks and Charles Samuels (and later Edward Hammond). Robinson, the first tenor, was a 1911 graduate of Franklin College and an educator and musical director at many of the prominent churches in Indianapolis. He also performed in a neighborhood musical group with his childhood friend, the songwriter and composer Noble Sissle. Wallace Wolfolk, second tenor, matriculated at the Boston Conservatory of Music. During his tenure in Boston, he sang for the queen of England.

Clarence Hicks, bass, was an educator in the Indianapolis Public School (IPS) system. Charles Samuels, baritone, was a public school custodian and unfortunately became ill in 1935; he was replaced by Edward Hammond, a shoe shop owner. Harry Campbell, pianist, was a faculty member of the recently opened Crispus Attucks High School, where he taught mathematics and Latin. As a vocalist, in 1929 Campbell recorded the song "You'll Be Sorry Someday" for the Gennett Record Company with legendary barrelhouse pianist Herve Duerson.

If there were one occasion that could be etched in stone as the most defining event that galvanized the African American community and made the tremendous sacrifices endured during this decade worthwhile, it was the grand opening of the Walker Building. On Monday, December 26, 1927, the doors swung open, and African Americans, as proud as peacocks, dressed in their finest attire, slowly strutted through the doors. It was such a festive celebration that seemingly one could hear triumphant bells tolling on Indiana Avenue. The opening ceremony in the theater featured the Hollywood film *The Magic Flame*, starring Ronald Coleman and Vilma Banky, as well as Reginald DuValle's Blackbyrds Orchestra, Mary Singleton playing the "golden-voiced Barton pipe-organ" and the vaudevillian dance team Lovey and Shorty. Columbia University–educated attorney Freeman B. Ransom, general manager of Madam C.J. Walker Manufacturing Company, dedicated the building "to those who toil; those who think; those who love good music; good pictures, high class entertainment…to all races."

Besides the opulence of the theater, which contained a North African Moorish décor with Egyptian sphinx sculpture, Moorish arches, spears and monkeys, the splendid edifice also contained the Walker Casino, the Walker Beauty Shop, the Walker Coffee Pot and numerous professional offices for doctors, lawyers, accountants and businesses. Indiana Avenue residents felt great pride when they gazed at the wonderment of this great structure in their midst. In order to truly comprehend its historical significance, one must recognize the blood, sweat and tears invested by its namesake, Madam C.J. Walker, to make this magnificent event possible.

Born on December 23, 1867, in Delta, Louisiana, shortly after slavery was no longer legal, Sarah Breedlove worked the cotton fields of the bottom land, took in laundry to make ends meet and worked as a washerwoman in St. Louis, Missouri. It was in St. Louis where she received the hair-care formula in a dream that would eventually make her a millionaire. In the biography *On Her Own Ground*, written by her great-granddaughter A'Lelia Bundles, the following narrative appeared: "I was on the verge of becoming entirely bald," Sarah often told other women. Ashamed of the "frightful" appearance of her hair and desperate for a solution, she "prayed to the Lord" for guidance. "He answered my prayer," she vouched. "For one night I had a dream, and in that dream a big black man appeared to me and told me what to mix for my hair. Some of the remedy was from Africa, but I sent for it, mixed it, put it on my scalp and in a few weeks my hair was coming in faster than it had ever fallen out." After obtaining the same results on her daughter and her neighbors, she later told a reporter, "I made up my mind I would begin to sell it."

In 1912, during a campaign to raise funds to construct the Senate Avenue Young Men's Christian Association located at 450 North Senate Avenue, Walker donated $1,000 to this cause, and at the time, no black woman was known to ever have contributed a sum of that size to a community-inspired project. Walker also made generous contributions to the Bethel AME Church located at 414 Vermont Street, where she held membership, and the Alpha Retirement Home of Indianapolis, located at 1840 Boulevard Place. She also donated thousands of dollars to organizations and educational institutions in several other cities. In July 1917, when a white mob murdered more than three dozen blacks in East St. Louis, Illinois, Walker joined a group of Harlem (New York) leaders who visited the White House to present a petition advocating federal anti-lynching legislation.

The poor little black girl born in the cotton fields of the Louisiana Delta and raised in abject poverty who discovered a hair-growing product that revolutionized the beauty industry did not forget her roots. As an entrepreneur, philanthropist, political activist and patron of the arts, she became one of the country's most powerful women of any color. Madam Walker invested her vast fortune in the uplift and betterment of her people, and her life was a splendid testament exemplified by the struggle, courage and perseverance that Indiana Avenue–area residents displayed during the twentieth century.

Before they could get booked in the clubs, some performers displayed their talent on the street, and the new Walker Building was a great place for them to attract attention. On a warm spring day in 1928, three young dancing singers performed on Indiana Avenue in front of the Walker Theatre to the delight of passing residents, who deposited coins in their coffers. The young men were Leonard Reed, James "Miff" Campbell and Orville "Hoppy" Jones. After gaining a little popularity with their sidewalk performances, they sought work in more permanent venues and named themselves the Peanut Boys. Simultaneously, Ivory "Deek" Watson was a member of a coffeepot band, a small musical aggregation that performed in front of business establishments on Indiana Avenue. Customarily, they placed a large coffeepot on the sidewalk and hoped that pedestrians would deposit coins in appreciation of their performance. Their repertoire included the music of Duke Ellington, Cliff "Ukulele" Edwards, Barney Rapp and McKinney's Cotton Pickers. This group distinguished itself from other acts on the Avenue by its soaring falsetto notes and ability to simulate wind instruments with their voices.

In 1931, after a series of personnel changes from different groups, Orville "Hoppy" Jones, James "Miff" Campbell, Ivory "Deek" Watson and Slim Green formed the Four Riff Brothers and performed together until Watson left to perform as a headliner. A few years earlier, Jerry Daniels, Bernie Mackey and Charlie Fuqua had formed a coffeepot band that featured soaring vocals and fancy dance steps. They performed at Fuqua's uncle's shoeshine stand in front of the Stutz Bearcat Automobile Factory on Capitol Avenue.

Shortly thereafter, Charlie Fuqua, Jerry Daniels and Bernie Mackey formed a trio and renamed themselves King Jack and the Jesters. They traveled the vaudeville circuit and had a radio show on WKBF-Cleveland. The group finally got a break and traveled to New York City, where they sought work along 125th Street in Harlem and in Lower Manhattan. However, a problem arose. Renowned bandleader Paul Whiteman had a vocal group that performed with his band called the King's Jesters, so the newcomers from the Midwest had to find another moniker. Legend has it that they brought the problem to their manager, Moe Gale, and he sat down at his desk, grabbed his ink pen to write and accidentally splattered ink on his desk pad—hence the name Ink Spots. In 1936, Daniels became dissatisfied with his paltry paycheck and left the group to return to Indianapolis. He was replaced by Baltimore native Bill Kenny, and three years later, the Ink Spots had their first million-selling record, "If I Didn't Care." The song, which would be their biggest hit, sold a whopping 19 million copies!

During the late 1920s and early 1930s, Indianapolis, and most of the country, experienced two major events that shook its economic foundation—Prohibition and the Great Depression. The first, Prohibition, was ratified in 1919 as the Eighteenth Amendment to the U.S. Constitution and placed a nationwide ban on the manufacture and transport of intoxicating liquors. On October 29, 1929, Black Tuesday, an economic panic struck Wall Street, sending financial reverberations that were felt in every sector of American

The Ink Spots, a popular musical group whose song "If I Didn't Care" is an all-time classic, began their career dancing for pennies and nickels in front of the Walker Theatre. *Courtesy of Indiana Historical Society.*

life and resulted in what came to be known as the Great Depression. Investors lost large personal fortunes as the stock market crashed. Millions of unemployed workers lined city sidewalks to get a bowl of soup and a piece of bread. The popular song that characterized this era was the melancholy tune "Brother Can You Spare a Dime?" People scraped and scuffled just to do what was necessary to survive.

In spite of the dismal economic forecast on Indiana Avenue, there was a reason to celebrate with the opening of Crispus Attucks High School in 1927 as the first and only public high school for African Americans in Indianapolis. The first principal of Crispus Attucks High School, Mathias Nolcox, recognized the fact that black students living in such a racist climate would have to receive a superb education in order to realistically compete economically with their white competitors. Therefore, Nolcox searched throughout the nation and recruited the finest African American educators and scholars available. One such scholar was Harold Brown, who was a music educator and band director. While at Crispus Attucks, Brown proved himself to be a dedicated music teacher and spent countless hours in the classroom and after school in rehearsals to ensure that his students were well prepared. As a consequence, Brown produced some of the finest musicians in the entire school system, many of whom graduated and became professional musicians. In the early 1930s, to honor Brown, a group of his former students organized an orchestra and christened themselves the Brown Buddies.

The Brown Buddies were an enterprising group of young musicians who employed a clever business strategy to maximize their popularity. Always well dressed and well groomed in finely tailored brown or white tuxedoes, these musicians synchronized each movement on the bandstand with the precision of a fine Swiss watch. The manner in which they captivated their audiences with their lively notes, zany antics and swift movements was their trademark and resulted in overflowing nightclubs

The Brown Buddies, Crispus Attucks alums who named themselves after their music teacher, Harold Brown, and toured the country. *Courtesy of Henry Woods.*

45

wherever they performed. The strength of these fine artists' performances was based on their previous experience and instrument mastery. The bespectacled Beryl Steiner was the accomplished alto saxophonist, Roger Jones and Renaud Jones (not related) were trumpet stylists and James "Step" Wharton was the pianist and arranger. Trumpeters Henry Woods and Herman Twines, saxophonists James Spaulding and Beryl Steiner, pianist Reginald DuValle and drummer Alvia Coleman were also members of the Brown Buddies. Many of these musicians had previously been associated with big orchestras in New York, Chicago and other large metropolitan areas. Steiner played with the Lucky Millinder, Jimmy Raschell and Tiny Bradshaw Orchestras and had recorded with Ethel Waters. Roger Jones had played with Cab Calloway and Don Redman, and Renaud Jones had played with Chick Webb, Don Redman, Willie Bryant and Doc Wheeler. Wharton had done arrangements and charts for Benny Goodman. In the March 17, 1934 edition of the *Indianapolis Recorder*, there is an advertisement announcing the grand reopening of Sea Ferguson's Trianon Ballroom featuring the Brown Buddies.

Chapter 4

The Avenue Returns to Life

During the 1930s, inside the dimly lit, smoked-filled juke joints, taverns and holes in the wall along Indiana Avenue, a new and exciting sound began to pierce the raucous atmosphere of merriment as the blues came to town. Only a decade earlier, a parade of female blues singers led by Ida Cox and Edmonia Henderson had passed through, but alas, they were actually out-of-towners who came to the Avenue to perform one night and left on the "next thing smoking" the following day. This phenomenon changed considerably as patrons of the Avenue unearthed precious jewels right in their own backyard.

One could casually stroll down the Avenue and, within one block, sample various genres of music that included ragtime, small bands and the blues. If one entered a hole-in-the-wall joint with broken chairs and table legs, greasy tabletops and the smell of cheap wine mixed with stale cigar smoke blanketing the air, one might see a pencil-thin pianist in a rough-dry suit sitting at an out-of-tune, rickety piano pounding out his latest blues tune on the ivories. At his side would be a tall, willowy, tan gentleman with pronounced American Indian features backing the pianist up with a gutsy guitar run. This duo was Leroy Carr and Francis "Scrapper" Blackwell, who came, saw and conquered Indiana Avenue.

Leroy Carr was born on March 27, 1905, in Nashville, Tennessee, only a stone's throw from Meharry Medical College and Fisk University on the city's north side. His father, John Carr, was employed as a laborer at Vanderbilt University. His mother, Katie Lytle Carr, was a domestic worker. At some

Leroy Carr, a hard-drinking blues singer who produced many great standards, died of alcoholism at an early age. *Courtesy of Duncan Schiedt.*

point during Carr's early childhood, his parents separated, and he and his mother first relocated to Louisville, Kentucky, and then to Indianapolis. During Carr's early years, he toured the Kentucky-Indiana region with a traveling circus, served a short stint in the United States Army, spent a year in the Indiana State Penitentiary for bootlegging alcohol, got married and had a daughter. To maintain his young family, he was employed at the Kingan's Meat Packing Plant and worked there for several years. In the early 1920s, Carr met blues guitarist "Scrapper" Blackwell. Carr and Blackwell became permanent fixtures in many establishments, on and off Indiana Avenue. Word of their musical genius spread like wildfire, reaching the offices of the Vocalion Record Company in New York. The Vocalion agents quickly scrambled to Indianapolis

Francis "Scrapper" Blackwell, Leroy Carr's accompanist who died years later in a fight in an alley. *Courtesy of Duncan Schiedt.*

to witness the new blues phenomenon and, without much resistance from Carr and Blackwell, immediately signed them to a contract. "How Long, How Long Blues" was their first release with Vocalion in 1928. The song was an instant blockbuster and prompted many wannabe blues singers from neighboring cities and states to try their luck at singing the blues.

Francis Hillman "Scrapper" Blackwell was born on February 21, 1903, in Syracuse, North Carolina, to Payton and Elizabeth Blackwell. He was African American and Cherokee and had fifteen siblings in his household. His family relocated to Indianapolis when Blackwell was quite young. He may have received his earliest musical influence from his father, who played the fiddle. Blackwell taught himself to play the guitar and reportedly built his first guitar from cigar boxes, wood and wire. Widely regarded as a reclusive individual who exhibited noncompliant and moody tendencies, little is known of Blackwell before he met Carr and made the hit record.

Sadly, as fate would have it, both Carr and Blackwell experienced unfortunate circumstances that led to their early deaths. First, during Carr's heyday of immense popularity and skyrocketing record sales, he developed a serious drinking problem that caused cirrhosis of the liver that ultimately killed him. Ironically, Carr's last recording was entitled "Six Cold Feet in the Ground," an eerie premonition of his final curtain call. Carr was thirty years old when he died on April 29, 1935. After Carr's death, a remorseful Blackwell took a twenty-year hiatus from recording only to reappear in June 1958 when he recorded for Colin C. Pomroy on the Collector Label—it was not released until a decade later in 1968. He was just beginning to reignite his musical career when he was shot and killed in an alley in Indianapolis in 1962.

In contrast to the rowdy, boisterous saloons and barrelhouses along Indiana Avenue that featured performers like Carr, Blackwell and other blues hollerers and shouters, there was a more refined, sophisticated genre of music that developed just off the Avenue in the homes of the African American upper class. Many socialites of the black elite regarded the blues as uncivilized and uncouth, a painful reminder of their not-so-distant southern past and slavery. They longed for a more European-oriented form of music. This form of music, called classical, served as a delineator between the more affluent neighborhoods and the impoverished black slums of the uneducated and unpolished masses. Although there is no documentation in newspaper accounts or oral histories, it is very likely that some of the singers of classical European music may have ventured onto the Avenue to experience that exciting type of music and entertainment.

The actual miles between those rowdy and boisterous barrelhouses, saloons and taverns on the Avenue and the glitzy and sophisticated atmosphere of the "Great White Way" of New York City may have been great in number, but for one Indianapolis musical star, it was a matter of masterfully navigating his career and traveling each segment deliberately, precisely and with carefully calculated speed. This star of the future was Todd Duncan.

Robert Todd Duncan was born on February 12, 1903, in Danville, Kentucky. In the 1910 federal census of Kentucky, he is identified as living in the household of his grandfather, Owsley Cooper, and mother, Anna Cooper Duncan. In his early childhood, he and his mother moved to Somerset, Kentucky, where he attended Davis Chapel African Methodist Episcopal Church and sang in the choir. During this period, he received daily music lessons from his mother, who was an accomplished pianist. In 1916, he and his mother relocated to Louisville, Kentucky, where he attended the segregated black high school that was associated with Simmons University. Finally, he and his mother moved again to Indianapolis, where he attended Shortridge High School.

Duncan later entered Butler University, where he focused primarily on music and excelled in the classroom. He received his Bachelor of Music degree from Butler in 1925 and later attended the College of Fine Arts in Indianapolis, where he continued his study of voice and music theory. Duncan then traveled to New York, where he matriculated at Columbia

Todd Duncan, a Butler University graduate selected by Ira Gershwin as his first Porgy in the opera *Porgy and Bess*.

University and received his master's degree in music in 1930. In 1931, he accepted a professorship in voice and music theory at Howard University in Washington, D.C. There, he met and married Gladys Jackson, a public school teacher; they had one son.

From Washington, he went to New York City, where he auditioned for the leading role of Porgy in George Gershwin's blockbuster black opera *Porgy and Bess*. After having auditioned more than one hundred baritones for the role, Gershwin listened to Duncan and immediately terminated the audition process. Gershwin coyly approached Duncan and asked, "Will you be my Porgy?" The musical debuted on Broadway on October 10, 1935, and Duncan appeared in almost two thousand performances.

Duncan later appeared as Escamillio in Bizet's *Carmen* with the New York City Opera Company. He was also cast in such Broadway productions as *The Sun Never Sets* (1938), *Cabin in the Sky* (1940) and *Lost in the Stars* (1949), as well as in the films *Syncopation* (1942) and *Unchained* (1955).

While performing on Broadway for twenty-five years, Duncan also sang more than two thousand recitals in fifty-six countries. He received an honorary LHD degree from Valparaiso University, Indiana, in 1950 and in 1958 earned a Doctor of Music degree from Central State University, Wilberforce, Ohio. After many years of outstanding performances, Duncan died quietly of a heart ailment in his Washington, D.C. home in 1998. The great musical talent that was watered and nurtured in Indianapolis bloomed magnificently in New York and around the world.

During the third and fourth decades of the last century, many entertainers, regionally, nationally and internationally known, appeared in establishments along Indiana Avenue. The *Indianapolis Recorder* is replete with articles of great entertainers who paid visits to the Avenue. Stars of celestial magnitude such as Fats Waller, Count Basie, Duke Ellington and Louis Jordan found occasion to perform in Indianapolis, on and off the Avenue, for its throng of supportive and appreciative fans. Because of the immense fame and earth-shaking name recognition of these stars, one might logically conclude that they would cast a long shadow over the local entertainers and siphon off their popularity. But such was not the case. There were local bands and orchestras that were wildly popular, according to the glowing reviews they received from the *Indianapolis Recorder* on a weekly basis. One such orchestra that distinguished itself was Buddy Bryant and His Gentlemen of Jam, featuring Frank Reynolds.

Bryant A. Hurd was born on April 30, 1909, in Milton, Tennessee, to Dudley and Anna Hurd. Early in his youth, he adopted the moniker "Buddy," which followed him throughout his professional career. He dropped Hurd as his last name and substituted his first name because it had greater public appeal. After high school, he was "bitten by the music bug," picked up the saxophone that he had studied in his youth and embarked on a career in entertainment. In the early 1930s, he organized a band composed of musicians from Milton, Tennessee, and neighboring small towns. The Buddy Bryant Band toured St. Louis, Missouri, and many small towns in southern Illinois and Indiana, playing to appreciative audiences.

In 1933, Bryant married Hazel M. Lanum of DuQuon, Illinois, and they later relocated to Indianapolis, whereupon he met Sea and Denver Ferguson, who helped establish his career on the Avenue. He recruited some of the finest musicians in the Midwest and renamed his aggregation Buddy Bryant and His Gentlemen of Jam. The *Indianapolis Recorder* documented their numerous performances at establishments such as Joe Mitchell's club, the Mitchellyn Tavern; Denver Ferguson's Royal Palm Gardens; Sea Ferguson's Cotton Club; the Walker Casino; and the IBEW Union Hall. On July 23, 1943, when he was thirty-four, Buddy was drafted into the United States

Patrons celebrating at Joe Mitchell's Mitchellyn Tavern circa 1940. *Courtesy of Edward Mitchell.*

Army during World War II. In the army, he entertained the troops with his music. After his discharge, Bryant, an avid camper and sportsman, enjoyed annual hunting and fishing trips to Wisconsin and Canada, but he was never far away from his first love: music. He had a day job at the Veterans Administration Hospital for eighteen years and died in June 1993 at the age of eighty-four. Bryant was definitely a musical force on Indiana Avenue during his heyday.

The great migration of African Americans from the South to the North after World War I allowed for the integration of many different African-derived art forms from different regions of the South to merge into a new expression of African American creativity. This merging of a unique creative experience was quite evident in the development of dance. From the exotic rhythmic movements displayed in worship ceremonies in West Africa to the buck and wing dances performed by slaves on the plantations of the South and the cakewalk performed by traveling minstrel shows of the 1800s, dance has been a way to express freedom from convention and escape from reality.

Bill "Puddin'" Pierson and Bobby Campbell, dancing duo that tap-danced its way to stardom from Los Angeles to New York's Broadway. The two performed at the famed Apollo Theater in Harlem, New York. *Courtesy of William Pierson Jr.*

Many of the nightclubs and other entertainment venues on Indiana Avenue from the 1920s until its death in the 1970s featured fast-stepping dancers to inject excitement and intensity into their shows. Some of the most popular "hoofers," as dancers were called, were the Four Thunderbolts, which consisted of Bill "Puddin'" Pierson, Walter Green, Henry Hicks and Bobby Campbell. These dancers appeared in almost every venue on the Avenue and traveled throughout the country to display their showmanship. Bobby

Campbell performed on the bill with vocalists Pearl Bailey, Sister Rosetta Tharpe and Billy Eckstein and bandleader Lucky Millinder when they came to town. Another great pair of Indiana Avenue hoofers was the dance team of Leonard & Leonard, which consisted of Leonard Chester Thomas and Paul Leonard Harrell. In July 1955, Indiana Avenue history was made when this dancing duo appeared at the Palladium Theatre in Sydney, Australia. The local newspaper ran this review: "Leonard & Leonard, one of the few

Leonard & Leonard, sensational Indiana Avenue dancing duo that performed on the Ed Sullivan show *Toast of the Town* and toured the world, receiving rave reviews in Australia. *Courtesy of Lockefield Civic Association.*

top-line dancing duos in the world, have scored a sensational success with Sydney audiences. Now featured in 'Harlem Blackbirds' at the Palladium, this brilliant pair has evoked wildly enthusiastic applause from packed houses in the last three and a half weeks. There's nothing sophisticated about the dancing of these boys. They're real negro and proud of it." On October 12, 1958, Leonard & Leonard appeared on the Ed Sullivan show *Toast of the Town* and received rave reviews in New York newspapers.

The entertainment establishments along Indiana Avenue showcased many performers who would eventually leave town and gain worldwide recognition. The vaudeville duo of Buck 'n' Bubbles was no exception. Ford L. Washington (Buck) was born in 1905 to Aba and Jennie Washington in Louisville, Kentucky. John William Sublett (Bubbles) was born in 1903 to Katie and John William Sublett Sr. Early in his life, Bubbles's family relocated to Indianapolis. In 1919, he met Washington and formed their song-and-dance team, with Buck playing the stride piano and singing while Bubbles tap-danced. The duo appeared in the Ziegfeld Follies of 1931, and the men were also the first black artists to appear at the Radio City Music Hall in New York City. On November 2, 1936, they performed live in the inaugural program of the world's first live telecast at Alexandra Palace, London, England, becoming the first black artists to perform on television.

In 1935, Bubbles was chosen by George Gershwin to create the role of Sportin' Life in his opera *Porgy and Bess*. Buck also appeared in Hollywood films of the late 1930s and 1940s, including *Varsity Show* in 1937, *Cabin in the Sky* in 1943 and *A Song Is Born* in 1948. He also continued to make television appearances, one of his last being on a musical episode of *The Lucy Show*, which, in addition to Bubbles, also guest-starred Mel Torme. Bubbles died in New York on May 18, 1986.

One of the early guitarists who carved a name for himself on Indiana Avenue hailed from the rolling hills of Kentucky. William Arthur Gaither was born to Samuel O. Gaither and Bertha Kennison Gaither on April 21, 1910, in Belmont, Kentucky. In the early 1930s, he performed with both Leroy Carr and Scrapper Blackwell. Later, he recorded with Carr under the name Leroy's Buddy. Upon Carr's death in 1935, Gaither developed a musical relationship with stride pianist George "Honey" Hill as a lyricist. Among Gaither's recordings are "After the Sun's Gone Down" and "Life of Leroy Carr." The most popular hit was "Champ Joe Louis," which was recorded on June 23, 1938, the day after the famous rematch between boxers Joe Louis and Max Schmeling.

In 1940, Gaither returned to Kentucky and opened a music shop called Donald Duck Records, where he operated a radio and jukebox repair service. Previously, he had recorded on Decca Records but moved to Okeh Records, where he adopted the moniker "Little Bill" Gaither. He called himself "Little Bill" as an expression of respect for the label's established blues warbler, "Big Bill" Broonzy.

In 1942, Gaither was drafted by the United States Army and became a member of the African American First Battalion of the Twenty-fourth Infantry Regiment. Gaither's unit experienced fierce combat in the Solomon Islands and was later assigned to the island of Saipan, where they were responsible for capturing Japanese soldiers who had yet to surrender. This combat experience proved to be a traumatic ordeal for Gaither; when he returned home, he suffered from a nervous condition that caused him to end his music career. In 1948, back in Indianapolis, he got married, was employed as a manual laborer at a cafeteria and also repaired jukeboxes, pop machines and furnaces along Indiana Avenue. "Little Bill" Gaither died on October 27, 1970.

Contemplating its artistic totality, one could conclude that entertainers of all kinds constituted a galaxy of stars that paraded up and down Indiana Avenue, performing before ecstatic patrons who enjoyed every second of their performances. Truly, they were the best of the best. Occasionally, one star would gather up enough cosmic energy to enable it to burst out of its orbit and travel to distant planets, where a new constellation would benefit from its luminosity. One such star whose musical genius germinated on the Avenue but whose artistic flower reached full bloom on the East Coast was Trevor Bacon.

Trevor Bacon was born circa 1907 in Roaring Spring, Kentucky, located in Trigg County, to Jim and Ora Bacon. He was the third of four children according to the 1920 federal census. At an early age, young Trevor picked up the banjo and taught himself to play, acquiring a great deal of attention from music lovers in his small town. Later, he graduated to the guitar and really began to explore the melodic depths of this instrument while also attending the local school and doing his chores around the house. In his teen years, the family moved to Indianapolis in the early 1920s, and Bacon discovered the music scene of Indiana Avenue. Cautiously venturing onto the Avenue and auditioning for several bands desperately in need of a string sideman, Bacon held his own with his masterful playing of the banjo and guitar. However, what really caught the attention of these bandleaders was not only the skillful execution on his instruments but also his silky smooth and tremendous

Trevor Bacon, a popular singer who traveled to New York and fronted some of its greatest orchestras. He recorded a song for returning servicemen from World War II that is a classic. *Courtesy of Trevor Bacon Jr.*

vocal range. After Bacon had performed with several bands as an instrumentalist and vocalist, the nationally renowned bandleader Lucky Millinder came to town for an engagement. Millinder was told by a local promoter to see a performance of Trevor Bacon, the young man with "that voice." After seeing Bacon perform, Millinder immediately signed him to a contract and took him on the road, with New York City as the final destination.

Arriving in New York City in the early 1940s, Bacon must have been amazed by the enormity of the skyscrapers, the quick hustle and bustle of big city life and the numerous entertainment venues in all boroughs of the city. For a young man from rural Kentucky, the initial experience of witnessing New York City must have been electrifying. However, it did not take long for Trevor to catch his breath, unpack his suitcase and make a fluid transition to life in the "Big Apple." Almost overnight, word of Lucky Millinder's new vocalist, the Naptown gent with that silky smooth vocal delivery, caught the eyes and ears of the New York press. Folks from far and near stormed the neighborhood nightclubs to witness this singing sensation. Bacon performed before standing room–only crowds in every major entertainment venue in Harlem, including Frank Schiffman's world-famous Apollo Theater.

Millinder decided to broaden the scope of his Broadway-style revue and thereby relieve some of the nightly performance pressure on Bacon. He added to the entertainment bill Sister Rosetta Tharpe, the blues/ gospel recording queen who was one of the top in the nation, as well as Peg Leg Bates, a South Carolina amputee who dazzled crowds wherever he performed by dancing with one leg and a wooden stump with remarkable agility. On twenty occasions, he appeared on the nationally popular Ed Sullivan television variety show *Toast of the Town*. Trevor recorded several hit records with the Millinder Orchestra, including "Big Fat Mama," "Are You Ready?" "Sweet Slumber," "Hey Huss" and "Deep in the Heart of Texas." His greatest hit was "When the Lights Go On Again (All Over the World)," a song that anticipated the joy and excitement that would result from the end of World War II.

After several years of performing and recording with the orchestra, Bacon followed Millender's lead saxophonist, Tab Smith, who left to organize his own orchestra. Although Bacon was a nationally renowned vocalist with greater name recognition than Tab Smith, the orchestra was forced to adopt the Tab Smith moniker because Bacon was still under contract with Millinder. With the Tab Smith Orchestra, Bacon recorded several great hits, including "You Lovely You" and "I'll Live True to You."

Sadly, at the height of his immense popularity, tragedy struck. En route to New York for an engagement, Bacon was killed in an automobile accident near Sumter, South Carolina, in April 1945. He was only thirty-eight years old. Entertainment icons and luminaries such as Duke Ellington, Cab Calloway, Ella Fitzgerald and Earl "Fatha" Hines paid their final respects at Indianapolis's Jacob Brothers Funeral Home. In New York, there was a tremendous outpouring of grief by his adoring fans at a memorial service as hundreds of people lined the Harlem sidewalks to bid farewell to Trevor Bacon. The cosmic burst of celestial energy that emanated from Indiana Avenue and soared through the high heavens to New York City had finally burned out and came crashing to earth. Trevor Bacon was gone, and two cities in America were in deep mourning.

Chapter 5

Out-of-Towners Shine on the Avenue

N ew Orleans has given the world of music many precious gifts. It is one of the birthplaces of jazz and home of the world-famous Mardi Gras, trumpeter great Louis Armstrong and the most delicious gumbo soup. One of the gifts that it presented to Indianapolis was William Thomas Dupree. Dupree was born to an African American/Cherokee mother and a Belgian Congolese father on July 4, 1908. By the time he was two years old, both his parents had died in a house fire. He was sent to the New Orleans Home for Colored Waifs, where Louis Armstrong had once lived. A self-taught pianist, Dupree was an understudy of the legendary "Tuts" Washington, who served as his father figure, and he was a "spy boy" for the Yellow Pocahontas tribe of Mardi Gras Indians (spy boys were members of a Mardi Gras Indian gang who run a block or so in front of the main body during the Mardi Gras parade to look for other potential encounters with other gangs; if spotted, the boys usually signal by whistling). Dupree sharpened his piano skills by playing in smoke-filled and whiskey-smelling barrelhouse establishments all around the city.

Dupree left New Orleans in the late 1920s and traveled to Detroit, where he worked as a short-order cook. There he met world heavyweight champion Joe Louis, who introduced him to boxing. Dupree won the Golden Glove lightweight championship and earned the nickname "Champion Jack." Later, he traveled to Chicago, where he teamed up with bluesman "Georgia Tom," whose given name was Thomas Dorsey. Dorsey later transitioned to religious music and penned the classic gospel standard "Precious Lord

Take My Hand." Then, heading southward to Indianapolis, Dupree went directly to Indiana Avenue, where he fell under the spell of Leroy Carr and "Scrapper" Blackwell. Occasionally he sat in for Carr on piano when Carr was on a drinking binge. According to the November 12, 1940 edition of the *Indianapolis Recorder*, Dupree was appearing at Sea Ferguson's Cotton Club.

Dupree was drafted into the armed forces during World War II, and he was trained as a cook. He spent two years as a Japanese prisoner of war. In his later years, his popularity increased exponentially when white college kids discovered the blues. Dupree traveled and performed in concerts around the world. Up-and-coming music stars like English guitarists John Mayall, Mick Taylor and Eric Clapton sought to record with him in order to gain some musical notoriety on the blues charts. During the 1970s and 1980s, Dupree relocated to Halifax, Nova Scotia, where he performed regularly; the local government commissioned a plaque in his honor. Occasionally, he returned to the United States and performed at the New Orleans Jazz and Heritage Festival. Dupree died of cancer in Hanover, Germany, on January 21, 1992.

Contemporaries of Trevor Bacon and William Thomas Dupree who also shone brilliantly in Indiana Avenue's resplendent constellation were the performers of the Hampton family. The patriarch, Clark Fielding "Deacon" Hampton, was born in Batavia, Ohio, circa 1880 to William and Elizabeth Hampton. He had one brother, William, who was three years his senior. Deacon received his early education in a military academy in Xenia, Ohio, where he concentrated his studies on music and art. In 1908, he married Laura Burford, and into this union, twelve children were born, all of whom were trained to play an instrument skillfully. The family eventually organized a band originally known as Deacon Hampton's Pickaninny Band, but the name was later changed to Deacon Hampton's Family Band because the former name suggested a stereotypical racist image.

Traveling throughout states such as Pennsylvania, West Virginia, Kentucky and Indiana, the band performed in all kinds of venues, including carnivals, tent shows, private parties, dances and fairs. The act contained lively dancing, comedy skits and various kinds of music such as the blues, country songs, polkas and jazz. In the late 1920s, the family traveled to California to seek its fortune on Hollywood's silver screen, prompted by the success of child-oriented film projects such as *Our Gang* and *The Little Rascals*. However, their attempts to gain a foothold in Hollywood did not materialize.

Weary and dejected, the family moved to Indianapolis in the late 1930s, whereupon they met the brothers Sea and Denver Ferguson, owners of Indiana Avenue's hottest night spots, the Cotton Club and the Sunset

Terrace, respectively. The Ferguson brothers booked the Hamptons in their entertainment establishments, and the family began to enjoy a period of stability and permanency during which the children concentrated on their education and put down roots. A few years later, sons Marcus, Russell, Maceo and Locksley "Slide" Hampton attended the McArthur Conservatory of Music and the Jordan College of Music at Butler University.

During World War II, several of the Hampton men were called into the armed service, temporarily breaking up the band. Their sisters sought employment at local defense plants to maintain their livelihood. After a while, the Hampton sisters returned to the entertainment arena and formed a quartet that included Aletra on piano, Virtue on bass, Carmalita on baritone saxophone and Dawn on alto saxophone. They sang, danced and played their instruments at many of the nightspots on Indiana Avenue. At the conclusion of the war, Duke Hampton, the eldest son, who played baritone saxophone, organized a hot "jump" orchestra showcasing the brass section. The seats of that orchestra were filled by some of the Avenue's finest musicians, artists such as saxophonists Alonzo "Pookie" Johnson and Bill Penick, trombonist/bassist Eugene Fowlkes and drummers Sonny Johnson, Dick Dickerson and Thomas Whitted.

In 1951, to boost national sales and circulation, the *Pittsburgh Courier* sponsored an entertainers' popularity contest. The rules of the contest required individuals to purchase subscriptions that would serve as votes for their favorite entertainer. An engagement at New York's famed Carnegie Hall would be the top prize for the winners. After weeks of voting by frenetic music fans across the country, the votes were tallied, and the Lionel Hampton Orchestra and the Hampton Family Band won top prizes. Overjoyed by their triumph and the anticipated national exposure, the Hamptons excitedly prepared for their engagement in the Big Apple. They borrowed money to purchase new uniforms and instruments, as well as an old school bus to transport them to New York.

In New York, on the night of their debut, the Hampton girls were busily dressing themselves and applying makeup in anticipation of their performance when a glum-faced stage manager knocked and entered the room. Hesitantly, he announced that the Hamptons would not go on stage because a problem had arisen. Totally shocked, the Hamptons asked why, and the manager replied that Lionel Hampton was extremely upset that a similarly named group would appear on the same engagement. Perhaps the crowd would be confused and presume that Lionel Hampton was related to the Hampton family. It was widely speculated that Lionel Hampton had heard reports about the Hampton family from music critics and feared the competition. Lionel's orchestra went on stage and performed the first set, receiving cordial applause, and then took a break.

During the intermission, as the Hampton girls were in tears, packing their uniforms for the return home, Duke Hampton knocked sharply at the door and shouted, "We're on!" Seemingly in a split second, the Hamptons rushed on stage, assembled their instruments and quickly began to play "The Push," their brother Russell "Lucky" Hampton's tune.

According to Dawn Hampton, "Lucky was playing his solo [on the tenor saxophone] and running back and forth on the stage, and people in the audience were bouncing and dancing in the aisles. Some of the folks rushed toward the stage and had to be held back by security. We had Carnegie Hall leaping!"

Hearing the pandemonium, Lionel Hampton rushed upstairs and stood in the wings, watching the frenzied crowd's reaction to the Hamptons. He stomped his foot, sending his drink crashing to the floor, and went ballistic. He cursed out the stage manager and the representatives of the newspaper and had to be restrained from fighting. After regaining his composure, his orchestra went on stage and played his signature tune,

The Hampton sisters. These siblings dominated the music scene on the Avenue in the 1940s and 1950s. They recorded their first 78, "Hey Little Boy/My Heart Tells Me," on the Savoy Record label. *Courtesy of Indiana Historical Society.*

"Flyin' Home," for half an hour. Lionel Hampton had been upstaged, and he did not appreciate it. He felt that if any Hampton brought the house down, it should be *Lionel* Hampton!

In 1954, the Hampton sisters hit the proverbial "home run" when they signed a contract with Herman Lubinsky's Savoy label in Newark, New Jersey, to make a record. On a tour to New Orleans, accompanied by Hollywood comedian Mantan Moreland, the ladies stopped by a studio and recorded two great songs, "My Heart Tells Me," a slow-moving, sensual love ballad, and "Hey Little Boy," a fast-tempo, spicy jump number. Both songs were greatly appreciated by the regional radio audience and received considerable airplay. The Hamptons were guardians of Indianapolis's entertainment shrine for many decades from the 1930s until the late 1990s.

Although the Hampton family was replete with great musicians, some of whom left town and performed with the leading jazz orchestras of the time, there was one member who distinguished himself and stood head and shoulders above the rest. He was given the nickname "Slide."

Locksley Wellington Hampton was born on April 21, 1932, in Jeanette, Pennsylvania. He was the youngest of twelve children, all of whom played at least one instrument. In addition to receiving musical instruction in his home, he also attended the McArthur Conservatory of Music and was personally instructed by the owner, Ruth McArthur, and Eugene Franzman, woodwinds instructor. Although Hampton was right-handed, he was given a trombone set up to play left-handed.

In 1944, he played with the Duke Hampton Band, composed of his siblings, and eight years later, he performed with the Lionel Hampton Orchestra at Carnegie Hall in New York. In the late 1950s, he joined the Maynard Ferguson Band and not only performed but also arranged popular songs such as "Slide's Derangement," "Three Little Foxes" and "The Fugue." In the early 1960s, he organized the Slide Hampton Octet, which featured trumpeters Booker Little and Freddie Hubbard along with saxophonist George Coleman.

In 1968, Slide played with the Woody Herman Orchestra, and afterward, he resided in Europe for almost a decade. He returned to the United States in 1981 and became artist-in-residence at Harvard University. He held the same positions at the University of Massachusetts and DePaul University in Chicago. In 2009, he wrote a composition entitled "A Tribute to African-American Greatness," which honored Nelson Mandela, Barack Obama, Oprah Winfrey and Venus and Serena Williams.

Locksley Wellington "Slide" Hampton, trombonist extraordinaire and brother of the Hampton sisters, recorded on numerous record labels and won two Grammys. *Courtesy of Locksley Wellington Hampton.*

In 1998, he won a Grammy Award for Best Arrangement Accompanying a Vocalist for "Cotton Tail," performed by Dee Dee Bridgewater, and in 2005, he won a second Grammy for Best Large Jazz Ensemble Album for *The Way: Music of Slide Hampton*, performed by the Vanguard Jazz Orchestra. He received a Grammy nomination in 2006 for his arrangement of "Stardust" for the Dizzy Gillespie All-Star Big Band.

Jimmy Coe, a saxophonist who fronted many bands and orchestras on Indiana Avenue and mentored many young musicians.

In 1938, a short, stocky seventeen-year-old lugging his saxophone case hurried into Sea Ferguson's Cotton Club to secure a gig at the hottest club on Indiana Avenue. A little hesitant because of the young man's youthful appearance, Ferguson agreed to an impromptu audition in the club's atrium as patrons sauntered through the doors. Nervously, young Coe opened and put his case on the floor, assembled his instrument, placed the mouthpiece to his lips and began to produce the most beautiful notes that someone of his young age could possibly blow. Totally astonished, Ferguson led the young man to the bandstand and introduced him to the Buddy Bryant Orchestra that was performing and sternly announced, "This is your new saxophonist!" This was the beginning of a long, successful career. James Robert "Jimmy" Coe was born in Tompkinsville, Kentucky, on March 20, 1921, to Mary Wilburn Coe and William Coe. Coe's family moved to Indianapolis when he was two years old.

Coe's earliest recollection of his household was the musical influence of his three-hundred-pound cousin, Lottie Williams, who would sing popular and gospel tunes around the house. His father, who played the violin, bought his son a small, three-quarters-size violin. They also had an old piano with pump pedals that young Coe banged on incessantly as a toddler. In his early teen years, Coe took his piano-playing skills to neighborhood house parties, and according to him, "I started learning tunes off that [piano], and I'd go to parties when I got to be fourteen or fifteen. When I started banging on the piano, I'd look up and everybody was gone, especially the girls. But I liked the piano and was thinking about being a piano player."

As a young teenager, Coe attended Crispus Attucks High School, the all-black high school that boasted a superb music department. Under the

From left to right: Hortense Bullock, Norman Merrifield, LaVerne Newsome, Russell Brown and Marian Burch—Crispus Attucks's music department instructors, circa 1940. *Courtesy of Crispus Alumni Museum.*

tutelage of such music scholars as Norman Merrifield, LaVerne Newsome, Harold Brown and Russell Brown, Coe chose to play the clarinet but later switched to the saxophone and was unable to get into the school band because of the intense competition. Undaunted by this experience, he joined a group of young, aspiring musicians who got their first professional gig in a nightclub in a white, economically depressed section of town called Ravenswood. In addition to Coe, the band's personnel consisted of Hugh Watts on drums, Filmore Hutchinson on trumpet and Erroll Grandy on piano. Although Grandy was legally blind, his musical ability was awesome. According to Coe, "He had perfect pitch, just uncanny. If you dropped a quarter on the floor, he could tell you what note that was!"

After Coe's successful audition at the Cotton Club, Sea Ferguson, owner of the club and real estate mogul, became his manager. Coe teamed up with saxophonist/clarinetist Cleve Bottoms, also known as Clemack, and the Wisdom Brothers, with Walter Wisdom on piano and Fred Wisdom on trumpet, and performed before sold-out audiences every night. Saxophonist Buddy Bryant took young Coe under his wing, and they went on to perform at Joe Mitchell's Mitchellyn nightclub. There Coe was able to gain invaluable experience playing with Indiana Avenue's finest musicians.

In 1941, Coe hit the big time and traveled to Kansas City to join the Jay McShann Orchestra, which featured an alto saxophonist named Charlie Parker. In April 1942, on tour at Harlem's world-famous Apollo Theater, Coe had the mammoth task of briefly replacing Parker during a few performances. Coe remembered Parker comically falling asleep on the front row as Coe took a solo before intermission. Coe left the McShann Orchestra in 1942 and joined Tiny Bradshaw's band, where he replaced Bobby Plater. Coe wrote baritone parts for everything in the Bradshaw book as he had previously done for the McShann book.

After Coe joined the United States Army in 1943, he was stationed in Fort Custer, Michigan, where he organized a band from the soldiers of the quartermaster outfit. They rehearsed daily and played dances on the base and a few private parties around town. Later, Coe was shipped overseas, where he met vocalist and trumpet player Lanny Ross, and they organized an Armed Forces Service Band that traveled all over the world to entertain the troops. They traveled aboard the USS *Holland*, which was the fifth-largest ship in the world. During the trips, they were preoccupied by the thought of being chased by German submarines as they performed. Coe spent the last three years of his army career entertaining troops in New Guinea and the Philippines.

After leaving the service, Coe briefly returned to the Tiny Bradshaw band in New York for a few sessions. Then he traveled to Indianapolis, where he met Wes Montgomery while playing at the Ritz nightclub. In the late 1940s, Coe formed an orchestra and got a performance and recording date at the Cotton Club in Cincinnati, Ohio, that stretched from 1950 through 1953. He accompanied a young Indianapolis vocalist, Flo Garvin, on her first record, "On the Outside Looking In/Let Me Keep You Warm," on Syd Nathan's King record label. Coe canceled his contract with Syd Nathan and headed for Chicago, where he recorded tunes on the States label, the most popular being "Run Jody Run."

In Indianapolis, after his stint in Cincinnati, Coe was employed by the United States Post Office during the day and at night performed in clubs on and off Indiana Avenue. Occasionally, he would back nationally known singers and shows that came to Indianapolis. During one of his last performances in 2003, Jimmy Coe performed with trumpeter Freddie Hubbard; saxophonists David Young, Alonzo "Pookie" Johnson and Keni Washington; and vibraphonist Billy Wooten at a jazz festival held at the Fountain Square Theatre on Indianapolis's south side. Jimmy Coe died on February 26, 2004.

If one were to circulate a questionnaire among the entertainment stars of Indiana Avenue that asked the question, "Who is the godfather of Indiana Avenue jazz—who instructed, nurtured and inspired the majority of the jazz entertainers?" the answer would be a resounding Erroll Grandy. According to jazzman Al Coleman, Grandy was such a fantastic musician that all the musicians liked to be around him. He taught them improvisation, chord changes and other finer points of music. He was blind and had perfect pitch. Affectionately known as "Ground Hog" by his entertainment contemporaries, Lucas Erroll Grandy was born on January 1, 1918, near Norfolk, Virginia, to Thomas and Mary Grandy. As a toddler, Grandy developed an immense affection for music and began playing church hymns on the family piano at the age of three. Years later, he created a local radio program that was concerned with church news and religious music. In 1936, his father, who was a minister, was called to the pulpit of Witherspoon Presbyterian Church. As a consequence, the family relocated to Indianapolis.

Erroll "Ground Hog" Grandy, considered by many as the "Godfather of Indiana Avenue jazz." Although legally blind, his hearing was superhuman. You could drop a quarter on the sidewalk, and he could identify the note.

Afflicted with a congenital eye disease that rendered him legally blind, Grandy did not let this disability stand in his way; he was the pianist/organist at his father's church and played at house parties throughout the city. As longtime Indiana Avenue resident Thomas Ridley remembered, "A house party wasn't a house party if Ground Hog wasn't singing and tickling the ivories; he was great!" Grandy's high school classmate Howard Pipes related that Ground Hog used to love to imitate Fats Waller by walking around Crispus Attucks High School hollering out, "Hotcha, Hotcha," one of Waller's favorite lines.

In 1940, Grandy entered the Jordan Conservatory of Music, now a part of Butler University, and graduated four years later with a bachelor's degree. After touring briefly with Jimmy Coe's Orchestra, Grandy ventured onto Indiana Avenue and performed at almost every nightclub located there with the Count Fisher Trio. The trio consisted of Grandy on organ, Fisher on drums and Chuck Bush on bass. Occasionally, Grandy was contracted to back up touring superstars like vocalists Billie Holiday and Dinah Washington and bandleaders Count Basie and Lionel Hampton.

What made Ground Hog so incredibly different from other jazz mentors was the fact that he could take you where you were and make you a much better musician. He actually influenced jazzmen on other instruments with his piano playing. "If you came through Ground Hog, you had to be ready for any engagement; he was a natural genius with perfect pitch and knew his chord instruction," commented close friend and confidant Mingo Jones. Grandy was the godfather and mentor of every jazz and popular music entertainer who performed on Indiana Avenue during the 1940s and 1950s. Stars like Wes Montgomery, Freddie Hubbard, Leroy Vinnegar, J.J. Johnson, Alonzo "Pookie" Johnson, Willis Kirk, Larry Ridley, James Spaulding, Virgil Jones, Everett Green and Flo Garvin owe a great deal to the influence of Erroll "Ground Hog" Grandy. "If you consider Indiana Avenue as the Black Jazz Conservatory of Music, then Ground Hog was the dean," related Willis Kirk. After suffering for years with various medical issues, Grandy died on June 12, 1991, at the Alpha Nursing Home in Indianapolis.

Some jazz historians visualized the Indiana Avenue jazz experience in shades of black and tan, but that was not always the case. There were other colors of the rainbow that did not have a problem going down on Indiana Avenue and jamming with their entertainment siblings. Some jazz artists were more concerned with their passion for jazz and developing their skills than the hue of their band mate's face. Benny Barth was one equal-opportunity jazz artist who judged folks by the content of their character rather than the color of their skin.

Ben Caldwell "Benny" Barth was born on February 16, 1929, to Lucy Caldwell Barth and Jacob Jackley Barth in Indianapolis. When he was barely five years old, his mother, who had a fascination with the stage, took him by his hand and marched him downtown to the Jack Bodrick Dance Studios, where he took tap dance and vocal music lessons. Dressed in short pants, knee-high stockings, a white shirt and a tiny cap perched atop his head, young Benny dazzled the class with his precise footwork and vocal ability. So impressed was Jack Bodrick with young Benny's showmanship that he persuaded his mother to allow him to perform live on stage between movies at the Keith Theatre. His signature song was the slightly risqué "Oh You Nasty Man Making Love on the Easy Plan."

When he was in kindergarten, his parents wanted to broaden the scope of his entertainment repertoire, so they presented him with an accordion, which he detested. "I played the accordion for a day or two then kicked it over into the corner and never played it again," he vividly remembered. In 1941, he was employed as a soda jerk at the Riviera Country Club, working behind the counter dipping ice cream and making malts and banana splits. While working, he would listen to the enchanting music emanating from the bandstand and pay considerable attention to the drummer. He was fascinated by the timing and precision that the drummer had to maintain in order for the other musicians to keep their beat. In unison, he would tap his plastic spoon on the counter in cadence with the drummer and make believe that he was on stage performing in front of the audience.

At home, he gathered pots and pans from the kitchen and designed a homemade percussion section, on which he practiced at night after work. When word of his fascination for the drums spread around the family, he was electrified with delight one night when he returned home from the country club. There sitting in the middle of his living room with an aura of sparkle and excitement was a brand-new drum set. His namesake, Uncle Ben Caldwell, had brought the gift so that the pots and pans could return to their rightful places in the pantry of the kitchen.

In order to sharpen his musical skills, Barth enrolled in the Indiana Music School and took drum lessons from Buck Buchanan. Buchanan was a veteran drummer who played in the pit orchestra at the Circle Theatre and at the roller rink in Riverside Amusement Park. In 1943, while a freshman at Shortridge High School, Benny played in the Barton Rogers Orchestra, which was composed of leading music students from several high schools.

They performed at proms and dances at Butler, Indiana and Purdue Universities, as well as at dinners and teas around town.

In 1947, Barth entered Butler University to major in music education but found time to travel to Indiana Avenue to seek gigs and sharpen his musical chops. He landed at the Ferguson Hotel, where saxophonist Buddy Parker headed a group that included Bill "Sugar" Lane on bass and Grandy on piano. He also played at the Comas Club, located on Indiana Avenue, with Harold Gooch on bass and Parker on saxophone. Then he moved a few blocks north and appeared at George's Orchid Room, with Max Hartstein on bass and Al Plank on piano.

In the early 1950s, Barth, along with Slide Hampton on trombone and piano and Larry Ridley on bass, worked with noted trumpeter Conte Candoli at Club Shaeferee in South Bend, Indiana, owned by baritone saxophonist Nanny Rachelles. Candoli and his brother, Pete, another noted trumpeter, were born in Mishawaka, Indiana, but were based in Los Angeles. Candoli returned home on a visit and hired Barth, Hampton and Ridley to perform at the Shaeferee.

Chapter 6

The Talent Keeps on Comin'

Another white musician who traveled to Indiana Avenue to showcase his wares and sharpen his skills as a drummer was Dick Dickinson. Richard "Dick" Dickinson was born to Ethel Vorhis Dickinson and Gordon Dickinson on January 2, 1928, in Emory, Georgia. A few years later, with his sister, Beverly, his family relocated to Petersburg, Indiana. He grew up in Petersburg, a small agricultural city in southern Indiana, and later attended the Columbia Military Academy in Columbia, Tennessee. As a child, his earliest musical influence was his mother, who took him to many theatrical presentations and exposed him to "every cultural event that she could." In 1939, they traveled to Evansville, Indiana, to see the Count Basie Orchestra in concert. Seven years later, he saw vocalist Billy Eckstein and his orchestra in Louisville, Kentucky.

In 1946, after graduation from high school, Dickinson joined the United States Army, served during the occupation of Japan and was discharged two years later. Returning to Indiana, Dickinson entered Indiana University with the intention of studying medicine and following in the footsteps of his father, who was a family-practice physician. However, after a semester of rigorous classes and mediocre grades, he slowly began to develop an interest in music. He sadly related, "My father was disappointed. I know he was disappointed, but he went with it."

In 1950, Dickinson transferred to Florida State University and found himself immediately captivated by the college jazz scene. He distinctly remembered hearing and seeing the three jazz personalities who would alter

Dick Dickinson was one of the many white musicians who found a loving home on the Avenue. He came of age playing with the Hampton family. *Courtesy of Mark Sheldon.*

his course of study and change his life forever. Saxophonists Charlie Parker and Cannonball Adderley and trumpeter Nat Adderley were those "game changers." Dickinson vividly recalled Nat Adderley walking down the street in Tallahassee whistling a Maynard Ferguson tune as a "kind of signal to say, 'Here I am.'"

Dickinson returned to Indiana University and quickly became a part of the college jazz scene. He met his roommate, bassist Max Hartstein, and they both joined trombonist David Baker to perform at many of the fraternity and sorority gigs. In a 2008 interview with *Nuvo* magazine's Andy Krull, he related, "We'd always have a jam session afterward. A name band could be playing for the students and the piano player would join in [during the session]; that's how it was back then."

After college, Dickinson moved to Indianapolis and immediately made a beeline to the jazz establishments on Indiana Avenue. He hooked up with the established drummer Benny Barth, who mentored Dickinson and got him his first gig on the Avenue. Of Barth, he reminisced, "He was a great drummer. He nurtured me and then let me fly away." Dickinson met the Hampton Family Band members vibraphonist/trombonist Duke, trombonist Slide and trumpeter Maceo. He frequently made weekend visits to their home at 529–31 Vermont Street, where the family occupied both sides of a double house, and joined the jam sessions in their large basement. Legend has it that the family patriarch, Clark "Deacon" Hampton, prepared a concoction of extremely sweet Kool-Aid in a washtub for the musicians. After a long session, the visitors would stagger to the gigantic washtub, refresh themselves and then return to the bandstand to continue playing. Some of the people Dickinson jammed with until the wee hours were guitarist Wes Montgomery, pianist Buddy Montgomery, bassists Leroy Vinnegar and Monk Montgomery, trombonist J.J. Johnson, saxophonist Bill Penick and drummer Willis Kirk.

Shortly before his death, Dickinson related his impression of the Avenue jazz scene. "Indiana Avenue is where I got my real comeuppance in learning about music. I learned that jazz was really created by black musicians and that the blues was a major component of jazz. I received a lot of support from black clubs and musicians. I still feel that anybody who has not played with black musicians doesn't know what's going on."

The jazz scene also welcomed female performers. Flo Garvin was a pivotal figure on Indianapolis's music scene. Beginning in the late 1940s and stretching into the early 1970s, the name Flo Garvin was synonymous with elegance and charm mixed with a dab of sophistication. Generating excitement and electricity on and off Indiana Avenue, this empress of song single-handedly set a standard of entertainment excellence that others who followed her were required to match. Garvin was instant magic according to many jazz lovers who frequented Indiana Avenue and Meridian Street. During a period in which rigid segregation laws restricted the visibility of African American performers by dictating which venues they could and could not perform at, Garvin battled courageously to open doors that had been slammed shut to her people; she was considered a trailblazer.

Born Florence Crawford on January 15, 1927, and raised by her grandmother in the Lockefield Gardens public housing development that bordered Indiana Avenue, young Flo was introduced to the world of music and entertainment while attending Crispus Attucks High School. She studied the violin under the watchful eye of her mentor, LaVerne Newsome, and was a bright, energetic student who enjoyed the challenges that music presented and the discipline that it instilled in her. Originally, she had not the foggiest notion that she would ever consider the world of entertainment as a career choice, but as fate would have it, that was exactly what happened.

Her initial foray into the world of entertainment happened as she walked from school toward Indiana Avenue on a sunny summer afternoon. As she fondly recalled, she bumped into a dear friend, Sarah McLawler, who was a budding pianist/organist and vocalist in her own right. McLawler explained to Flo that she was on the way to a rehearsal at Sea Ferguson's Cotton Club. She asked Flo to be her accompanist because the pianist, Millard Lee, was ill. Although underage, Garvin accompanied McLawler, auditioned for the vacancy and so impressed Ferguson that she was hired on the spot.

Flo Garvin is credited as one of the early performers to appear in previously segregated entertainment establishments. She had one of the first African American television programs in the early 1950s. *Courtesy of the Flo Garvin family.*

Flo married Sammy Garvin and left her professional collaboration with Sarah McLawler to sing in jazz venues along the Avenue. Ernie P's 440 Club served as a launching pad for her initial success and also as an entertainment school where Flo Garvin polished her rough edges, gained some confidence and began to believe in herself as an entertainer. She expanded her artistic boundaries as a vocalist and became quite successful. Her trademark was her soft, sultry alto that lifted a simple, slow-moving ballad to a height never imagined as she painted a beautiful musical portrait with her voice using phrasing and vocal clarity. While this metamorphosis was slowly taking place, word of her talent spread to other regions of the Midwest.

In 1952, backed by Jimmy Coe's Orchestra, Garvin appeared at the Cotton Club in Cincinnati, Ohio. She received rave reviews, and the one-week engagement developed into a five-year contract, which included her recording session with the King Record Company. Garvin's record "I'm On the Outside Looking In/Let Me Keep You Warm" was a regional bestseller. Her popularity was growing.

In the 1950s, Jim Crow—segregation along racial lines—was still the law of the land. Many hospitals, restaurants, department stores and other businesses had policies that denied admission to African Americans. Nightclubs were no exception. In many establishments, blacks could enter through the back door to sweep the floors and cook in the kitchen, but they certainly could not perform or be admitted as patrons. All this began to change thanks to the determination and intestinal fortitude of people like Garvin.

In 1951, Garvin thrilled Indianapolis television viewers by becoming the first local African American entertainer to appear on a WFBM (channel 6) music program, *Sentimental Journey.* The show was sponsored by the Bud

Gates automobile dealership. She was backed instrumentally by the young guitarist Wes Montgomery, Fender bassist Monk Montgomery, pianist Buddy Montgomery and drummer Sonny Johnson. They appeared on this program for thirteen weeks.

Then Garvin made history again in 1953 when she became the first African American entertainer to perform in white clubs on both Meridian and Pennsylvania Streets. Appearing at Wally Antess's Club 220, she took the club by storm. This event led to subsequent bookings at plush supper clubs like the Keys and Bolen's, both establishments on Meridian Street. Although enthusiastically received by appreciative white fans, she faced

Sarah McLawler, the daughter of a prominent minister, learned her craft in the church and proudly displayed it on Indiana Avenue. She recorded many great songs on the Vee Jay label.

racial problems every night. At the Embers, she was advised by management not to mingle with the patrons between sets—that she should quietly relax in the kitchen during intermission. She vehemently refused both advisements and maintained her dignity by conducting herself as she always had.

In addition to being a spectacular entertainer, Garvin was a trailblazer who opened doors so that many other African American entertainers could enter. The name Florence Crawford Garvin occupies a prominent position in the history of our local entertainment greats. Flo Garvin died on November 20, 2005, in Indianapolis.

The friend who introduced Garvin to the entertainment world, Sarah Alberta McLawler, was born in Louisville on August 9, 1926, to Vol William and Lela Yvonne Tillery McLawler. Her father was a Baptist minister and Greek and Hebrew scholar, and her mother was a housewife. Young Sarah amused herself by playing songs on the piano as she frolicked around the church. As a small child, her parents divorced, and her father went to Pittsburgh, Pennsylvania, to pastor a new church.

He left Sarah to live with her mother. In 1936, her mother became critically ill and died suddenly.

McLawler then moved to Pittsburgh to live with her father, and when he accepted the call to the pulpit of Corinthian Baptist Church, they came to Indianapolis. One evening, while she was playing piano in the church, the minister of music, Vestarine Slaughter, overheard her. Slaughter held a graduate degree in sacred music from Butler University and taught at Crispus Attucks High School; she was impressed with the quality of Sarah's sound and her fingering technique. She immediately approached Reverend McLawler and convinced him to permit Sarah to have music lessons. Amazingly, in a few months, Sarah had become adept enough to occasionally play piano for the church choir; she also performed in a church band at South Calvary Baptist Church with a classmate, bassist J.J. Johnson.

In 1939, McLawler entered Crispus Attucks High School and began music instruction with Norman Merrifield. She sang in the a cappella choir and girls' Glee Club and began to play the clarinet. Of Norman Merrifield, she stated: "He had a tremendous impact on all of us. He had a lot of personality, and the students were crazy about him, and he was a fantastic musician and didn't demand any more of you than what he could do himself. We had one of the best music departments in the state of Indiana." During her high school days, McLawler sang with the Gene Pope Orchestra, which featured Erroll "Ground Hog" Grandy on piano. She was entertained at school dances by the Montgomery Brothers, a group that consisted of Wes Montgomery on guitar, Buddy Montgomery on piano and Monk Montgomery on bass. Sarah graduated at the top of her class and was a member of the National Honor Society. Shortly after high school, McLawler ventured onto Indiana Avenue and performed at Sea Ferguson's Cotton Club along with her childhood friend and Crispus Attucks classmate Flo Garvin.

McLawler attended Fisk University in Nashville, Tennessee, and later joined and toured with the Lucky Millinder Orchestra. Eventually, she moved to Chicago, where she organized the all-female band the Syncoettes, which performed in many of the jazz hot spots on the south side. When this group disbanded, she relocated to New York, met and married concert violinist Richard Otto and performed in many of the city's jazz clubs. Later, Sarah and Richard signed a record contract with Vee-Jay Records. For many years, McLawler delighted audiences and appeared weekly at the Chez Josephine restaurant and jazz club in New York owned by Jean-Claude

Baker, the World War II adopted French son of movie star/dancer/singer/ activist Josephine Baker. McLawler released her second CD, entitled *Under My Hat*, on Doodlin Records in September 2010.

After Flo Garvin's pioneering success, many Indiana Avenue stars gained formidable exposure by performing in plush supper clubs with sparkling chandeliers and thick Persian rugs on Meridian Street and in the suburbs. However, most still regarded Indiana Avenue as home base and reserved their finest performances for adoring jazz aficionados in the clubs that dotted its corridor. One such star was pianist/alto saxophonist James "Jimmy" McDaniels, the second son of Charles A. and Willie Viola Selden McDaniels. He was born on January 23, 1929, in Vinesville, Alabama. His father, a music professor, encouraged his children to play instruments. As a youngster, McDaniels practiced the piano daily. He graduated from Fairfield Industrial High School, Miles College, the Toledo Bach Conservatory of Music and Indiana University, where he took graduate courses in music and psychology.

Known nationwide for his musical gifts, McDaniels performed and conducted with vocalists Cab Calloway, Nat King Cole, Mel Torme, Rosemary Clooney, Joe Williams, June Christy, Sammy Davis Jr., Nellie Lutcher and vibraphonist Lionel Hampton. In 1961, he recorded his only album, *Jimmy McDaniels*, and it was well received in the entertainment community. He is a member of the Indiana Performing Arts Hall of Fame and the Alabama Jazz Hall of Fame. McDaniels was a fantastic pianist, and Indiana Avenue loved him. McDaniels died on April 25, 2009.

Since its inception, Hollywood has had a passionate fascination with the stereotypical image of the big, black, smiling Aunt Jemima–esque maid who was unquestionably obedient and loyal to the plantation owner's family. She invariably provided the family with comfort and respect. In 1939, the image was advanced by the bandana-headed, wide-eyed Mammy role played by Hattie McDaniel in the Hollywood blockbuster *Gone with the Wind*. Mammy's whole purpose was the care and comfort of Scarlett O'Hara, played by Vivien Leigh. This image was introduced on television in the 1950 situation comedy *The Beulah Show*, first starring Ethel Waters in the title role and then Hattie McDaniel and, finally, Louise Beavers, who played the role until the show ended in 1952. The story line centered on a black maid who is unquestionably devoted to her white family.

From the late 1940s to the 1960s, this image was projected on the Indiana Avenue scene by the local entertainer Ophelia. Ada Ophelia Hoy was born on November 5, 1916, in Macon, Georgia. As a child, she worked as a domestic for a wealthy white family who treated her badly. From this traumatic experience, she developed an intense hatred of whites. In the early 1930s, she moved to Indianapolis and obtained a job at the Indiana State Fair singing popular blues songs. As longtime Indianapolis resident, Howard Pipes, remembered, "I saw Ophelia in the 1930s at the fair sitting on a bandwagon wearing a soiled white dress singing these lively, comical songs. Even though she laughed and smiled when she sung those songs, behind that smile you could see a lot of sadness."

A decade later, Hoy performed frequently at the Douglass Theatre at the Midnight Ramble talent show that was held every Saturday night. At the Midnight Ramble, singers, dancers, comedians and musicians performed after midnight until the wee hours of the next morning. Hoy sang with Flo Garvin, and this collaboration developed into a lifelong friendship, as Garvin regarded Ophelia as her big sister. On many mornings after performing, the women would go to a Chinese restaurant on Indiana Avenue to eat. According to Garvin, the three-hundred-pound Hoy had a tremendous appetite. "She'd eat a huge bowl of food, and I'd say, 'Ophelia that's too much food to eat,' and then she'd say, 'Well, I'm not eating any butter!'"

On various tour dates, Hoy performed with vocalists Ethel Waters and Louis Armstrong, bandleader Lucky Millinder and dancer Peg Leg Bates. Although she performed at many places on Indiana Avenue, including the annual Walker Theatre Christmas Show, her most memorable performances took place at the Playhouse Bar, Town & Country Lounge and the Brass Rail, which were white establishments. At these venues, she would dress like a Mammy type, with a polka-dotted bandana on her head, and sing risqué songs to the delight of the raucous audiences. Her signature song was "Nuts, Hot Nuts, Get Them from the Peanut Man." According to Garvin, the club owner insisted that Hoy don the costume and assume the obedient maid persona while she sang the bawdy songs. However, Hoy was an extremely proud woman who loved and respected Indiana Avenue and her people, but she needed to earn a living. Sadly, in her last days on earth, Hoy was a recipient of welfare and died on August 15, 1968, at Marion County General Hospital.

Indiana Avenue boasted many pioneers who made Indianapolis proud by putting the Avenue on the nation's entertainment map. One such personality was James "Step" Wharton, who was born to James and Bessie Wharton on July 31, 1916, in Cadiz, Kentucky. At an early age, he developed an intense interest in music. After his family moved to Indianapolis in the early 1920s, he was encouraged by his parents to learn to play the piano.

They purchased a player piano with rollers that played songs automatically by programmed rollers that operated the keys and produced music. He spent many long and exciting hours upstairs in his room practicing on his piano. His mother kept him there listening to the piano so he could learn to play by ear. His parents also contracted the services of Reginald DuValle, who provided piano lessons for their industrious son. Ultimately, Mrs. Wharton removed the piano rollers and let him play on his own.

"I would unlock the keys and watch them," Wharton confessed. "Pretty soon, I could play any piano roll." In retrospect, Step appreciated his mother's diligence. "A lot of times at school they sent for me to come down to play piano parts because I could read music. A lot of guys were playing but were untrained. They were good piano players, but they couldn't read shows and things." Wharton's mother was always concerned with his career choices. In the 1930s, when Wharton was a student at Crispus Attucks High School, he had a burning desire to play football, but his mother thought that he might sustain an injury that would end his music career. Wharton, however, rebelled and joined the football team rather than attend Mr. Harold Brown's band practice. During the season opener, Wharton caught the game-winning touchdown pass, and his name appeared in the sports section of the next edition of the *Indianapolis Recorder*. His mother saw the story and made his first football game his last. Mrs. Wharton marched him directly to Mr. Brown's music class to make sure that he would practice his instrument. After high school, Wharton joined the popular orchestra the Brown Buddies and traveled the country with this fine aggregation of superb musicians. In 1951, Wharton became the first African American male to host a television program on WFBM, channel 6. It was called *Steppin' with Step*, and it featured his piano playing and vocal skills and was sponsored by the Kirk Furniture Company.

Another musician trained at Attucks was James Louis Johnson. Johnson was the son of James Horace and Nina Geiger Johnson, born on January 22, 1924, in Indianapolis. His parents had opposing child-rearing philosophies, with the father being a strict disciplinarian who demanded absolute control and harsh punishment. His mother was a gentler and more understanding parent who nurtured the children in a positive environment. Johnson's parents attended separate churches; their children were required to attend both Baptist Sunday school with their father and Methodist services with their mother. Although Nina Johnson knew little about music, she nevertheless hired a piano teacher for the children. James Johnson was given the nickname "J.J." by playmates and began piano lessons

J.J. Johnson, considered one of the top trombonists to perform on Indiana Avenue, left in the late 1940s and thrilled jazz aficionados on both coasts. *Courtesy of Kevin Johnson.*

when he was eleven years old. At school, he played the baritone saxophone for a short time but switched to the trombone when he was fourteen and formed a band with some of his friends. "We'd get together and just kind of jam," he told National Public Radio. "And [we] needed a trombone player, and so I tried the trombone out and got to fill the gap." He listened to other trombonists, including Fred Beckett and Dickie Wells. Johnson also played trombone in the Crispus Attucks High School band and with the Senate Avenue YMCA marching band.

In September 1941, Johnson ventured onto Indiana Avenue and got his first formal engagement with the Clarence Love Orchestra of Kansas City. In March of the following year, he joined the Snookum Russell Orchestra, with Ray Brown on bass, Fats Navarro, Tommy Turrentine and Herbie Phillips on trumpet for eight months. The band broke up in October, and Johnson returned home from its national tour. When Benny Carter visited Indianapolis a few days later, he was in need of a trombone player, and Johnson was recommended. Johnson remained with the Benny Carter Orchestra for the next two years, and in 1944, he traveled to Los Angeles and performed in the Jazz at the Philharmonic Concert. Over the next several years, on different occasions, he played with bandleaders Count Basie and Illinois Jacquet, trumpeter Dizzy Gillespie and saxophonist Charlie "Bird" Parker. Between 1949 and 1950, he recorded with trumpeter Miles Davis on the legendary *Birth of the Cool* sessions. "His association with Miles Davis was as significant in widening his socio-professional network as it was in expanding his stylistic horizons," wrote Joshua Berett and Louis G. Bourgois in their book *The Musical World of J.J. Johnson*. Johnson was elected to the Down Beat Jazz Hall of Fame in 1995 and retired from performing in 1997.

"I'm just weary of being a slave to the trombone," he told Ed Enright of *Down Beat* magazine. J.J. Johnson died on February 4, 2001, in Indianapolis.

Leroy Vinnegar was another fabulous Indianapolis jazz musician of this period, born on July 13, 1928. His parents were Aaron and Helen Vinnegar. As a child, he would amuse himself by playing the piano around the house, but early on, he never took the instrument seriously. Some would tease him that his large hands were an impediment to his learning to play the piano. Eventually, Vinnegar was introduced to the bass and was instructed by legendary pianist Erroll "Ground Hog" Grandy, who was Vinnegar's primary teacher and mentor. Grandy taught him concepts and techniques of playing bass lines by rote and hired him on his gigs. Other Indiana Avenue musicians began to hire him in their groups, and he became recognized for his big-band sound.

In 1952, at the age of twenty-four, Vinnegar moved to Chicago and won a seat as the house bass player at the Beehive Jazz Club. He backed local and touring artists, including saxophonist Charlie Parker. Two years later, he headed to Los Angeles. There, he gained a considerable reputation among jazz aficionados with his unique style of playing the bass—a big-band sound and steady walking bass accompaniment and solo patterns. Instantly, he became a jazz sideman favorite and performed with stars such as trumpeters Chet Baker and Shorty Rogers; saxophonists Herb Geller, Serge Chaloff, Art Pepper and Harold Land; and pianists Russ Freeman and Carl Perkins, who was also originally from Indianapolis.

Leroy Vinnegar's trademark was the rhythmic "walking bass line." Known as "the Walker," he appeared on André Previn and Shelly Manne's classical jazz LP *My Fair Lady*. It was the first million-selling jazz LP. *Courtesy of Portland State University.*

Vinnegar considered Erroll Grandy and Carl Perkins geniuses and his favorite piano players. The highlight of his extensive recording career, in which he either recorded or appeared on 142 records, was his collaboration with André Previn and Shelly Manne on the bestselling album *My Fair Lady*, a jazz version of tunes from the Broadway show. The album was released in 1956 on Lester Koenig's influential West Coast–based Contemporary Records jazz label. This was the first million-selling jazz album.

In 1957, Vinnegar made his debut as a jazz bandleader with his release of the *Leroy Walks* album, which was followed by *Leroy Walks Again* six years later. Both albums were critically acclaimed and featured Vinnegar's ability to walk his instrument through intricate bass lines. He then teamed up with saxophonist Teddy Edwards in the early 1960s and produced the classic *Teddy's Ready*, with Joe Castro on piano and Billy Higgins on drums, and later with pianist Les McCann and saxophonist Eddie Harris on their classic album *Swiss Movement* in 1969.

Because of health issues, Vinnegar relocated to Portland, Oregon, in 1986, where he became a central figure on the local jazz scene and added an element of authenticity to its jazz ambiance. He performed at many of the jazz clubs and restaurants around town and attracted the attention of up-and-coming jazz students. They frequently sought him out for technical instruction and lessons in jazz history. "Vinnegar was one of the mainstays of jazz all over the world. All I can do is think about the happiness he brought to people when he was playing. Every time he played jazz at the Opus Club, the place was packed and it was stomping. You could always count on him to be swinging, and that's what jazz is about. Let me put it this way: jazz equals swing; swing equals Leroy Vinnegar." This statement is from Dick Berk, jazz drummer who played with the great Billie Holiday and later worked with Vinnegar in Portland.

In honor of Leroy Vinnegar, the Oregon legislature proclaimed Leroy Vinnegar Day on May 1, 1995, in a special ceremony at the state capitol. He was installed as the first inductee into the Oregon Jazz Society Hall of Fame in 1998. Vinnegar died on August 2, 1999, in Portland, and in honor of his great contributions to jazz and his legacy, Portland State University established the Leroy Vinnegar Jazz Institute.

Chapter 7

Along Come the Montgomery Brothers

It was extraordinary for one family to have three members who were supremely gifted on their respective instruments, but the Montgomery brothers were beyond ordinary. They were among the best the Avenue offered, and their popularity was well documented. Whether in articles in the *Indianapolis Recorder*, on posters nailed on telephone poles or by word of mouth, the hometown Montgomery brothers were the toast of Indiana Avenue.

The oldest, William Howard "Monk" Montgomery, was born in Indianapolis to Frances Arrington and Tom Montgomery on October 10, 1921. Jazz historians credit him with being the first electric bassist of significance to introduce the Fender Precision Bass in 1951. He began his journey into the world of jazz after the success that was enjoyed by his brother Wes. From 1951 to 1953, Monk played with the Lionel Hampton Orchestra and then worked with his brother vibraphonist Buddy Montgomery, saxophonist Alonzo "Pookie" Johnson and drummer Robert "Sonny" Johnson in the Montgomery-Johnson Quintet. In 1951, they backed song stylist Flo Garvin on her program *Sentimental Journey* and became the first local African Americans to appear on Indianapolis television. In 1955, Monk moved to Los Angeles, California, where he formed the Mastersounds, which included Richie Crabtree on piano, Benny Barth on drums and his brother Buddy, who joined him on vibraphone. The group performed together until 1960. Monk recorded several albums with his brothers, including *The Montgomery Brothers Plus Five Others*, *George Shearing and the Montgomery Brothers*,

The Montgomery Brothers in Canada and *The Wes Montgomery Trio*. Also, he played with the Cal Tjader group from 1966 until 1970 and also played with the Red Norvo Trio. In his final years, he founded and was active in the Las Vegas Jazz Society and was planning a World Jazz Festival. Monk Montgomery died of cancer in Las Vegas on May 20, 1982.

Charles "Buddy" Montgomery was born on January 30, 1930, in Indianapolis. The youngest brother of jazz performers Wes and Monk Montgomery, he began his professional career in 1948 after his brother Wes taught him chords by illustrating them on his guitar and having Buddy repeat them on the piano. He also attended the Arthur Jordan Conservatory of Music, where he studied music theory. Buddy toured with Big Joe Turner's Orchestra and later teamed up with trombonist Slide Hampton, then joined the Montgomery-Johnson Quintet, which included his brothers, as well as Alonzo "Pookie" Johnson and Robert "Sonny" Johnson, who were not related. In 1955, Buddy was in Los Angeles with Monk and the Mastersounds. They recorded *Introducing the Mastersounds*, *The King and I* and *Kismet* in 1960. Shortly after the Mastersounds disbanded, he performed with Miles Davis.

In the early 1980s, Buddy moved to Oakland, California, where he recorded new material and played with the Riverside Reunion Band, with Charlie Rouse on tenor saxophone, David "Fathead" Newman on baritone saxophone, Bobby Hutcherson on vibraphones and Marlena Shaw on vocals. A new version of the band featured Buddy on vibes, Jimmy Heath on tenor saxophone, his brother Albert "Tootie" Heath on drums and Barry Harris on piano. The reorganized group made its first public appearance on Sunday evening, September 19, 1993. They recorded an album in honor of Thelonius Monk entitled *Mostly Monk* on September 20, 1993, at Fantasy Studios, Berkeley, California. Buddy died on May 14, 2009, in Palmdale, California.

If there were precious jewels showcased in the hot and lively jazz venues on Indiana Avenue during the 1950s, then Wes Montgomery was the most priceless display among them. Like his brothers, John Lesley Montgomery was also born in Indianapolis, on March 6, 1923. He later adopted the moniker "Wes" and carried it throughout his life. Although he attended Crispus Attucks High School and was exposed to arguably the best music department in the Indianapolis Public School system, Wes did not receive any formal music training. This lack of training rendered him unable to read chord symbols or notations throughout his musical career. When Wes was twelve years old, his older brother Monk brought him a four-stringed tenor guitar on which he would strum from time to time, never taking the instrument too seriously. However, when Wes was nineteen, his appreciation of music would take a "turn toward the best" as he, by chance, heard the recording entitled "Solo Flight" by the great jazz guitarist Charlie Christian. Of that life-changing experience, Wes commented, "When I heard Charlie Christian, I didn't know what to think because I hadn't heard anything like that. I hadn't even heard French guitarist Django Reinhardt yet. Christian got me all messed up."

Inspired by his Charlie Christian–induced epiphany, Wes rushed to a pawnshop on Indiana Avenue and purchased a brand-new guitar and amplifier. He immediately discovered that playing the guitar required a great deal of wisely invested time and total commitment. Wes may have initially assumed that all he would have to do was to strum a few strings on the guitar, and a series of beautiful notes would resonate, but he soon dismissed that pipe dream and realized that he would have to master the instrument in order to be successful. "I didn't know any of the fundamentals or nothing," he said. When he picked up his guitar to practice a few chords, he lamented that it "was more trouble than I'd ever had in my life! I didn't want to face that. It let me know where I really was. It was disappointing."

Fortunately, the future Indianapolis jazz great eventually discovered that the process was inspiring as well. He recalled, "With a little drive within myself, I stayed on the inspiring side. Because there's been so many cats that buy a guitar, pluck around for a week and then it's hanging up. He'll never touch it no more. It only means that it crosses your mind first as a thought. When you come to producing, this is another side altogether. But this is the sincere side of it. Either you will or you won't."

Wes later purchased another guitar and amplifier in order to produce a more powerful, intense sound, and this was directly related to the unorthodox playing style that he developed in his quest to master the instrument. But what was considered beautiful chords to him was experienced as excruciating, nerve-wrecking noise to his irritated neighbors. He related, "I'm sitting in my house, playing, you know, happy when I used my brand-new amplifier, I guess I didn't think about the neighbors. Soon they started complaining pretty heavy." His exasperated wife, Serene Montgomery, chimed in and demanded that he "kindly turn that thing off." What happened next changed the sound of the jazz guitar forever. "So I laid my pick down on the amplifier and just fiddled around with the thumb, and I said, 'Is that better?' 'Oh yes,' she says, 'that's better.' So I said, 'I'll play like this 'til I get ready to play out and then I'll get me a pick.' Well, that wasn't easy either because I found out that I had developed the thumb for playing so that when I got ready to work my first job, I picked up a pick and I think I must have lost about fifteen of them!" He continued, "I just didn't realize that I had to develop my pick technique, too. So I said, later for the pick. I was just playing for my own amusement, so it was great. See, I couldn't hear the difference in the sound as it is today, so I figured O.K., I'll just use my thumb."

Wes's fascination with his newly purchased guitar and amplifier and foray into the world of jazz proved to be infectious to other family members. His younger brother Buddy began to tinker around on the piano, and Monk bought a bass from a pawnshop on Indiana Avenue and immediately began to jam. Jazz became a family affair. "Around 1945–46, we used to have jam sessions up to my mother's [house] in Indianapolis every Sunday. Erroll Grandy knew all about the chords and everything, and soon my brothers got tired of watching, and Monk went out and got him a bass and soon got to playing. Buddy started playing the piano, and soon it got to be a regular thing." Wes began to perform at small clubs along Indiana Avenue, including the popular 440 Club. Initially, he was cordially received by the music-loving public, but no one was breaking the doors down to hear him play. According to Indiana Avenue song stylist Flo Garvin, "Montgomery used to come into the 440 Club, and folks would look up and say, 'Oh hell, here comes Wes lugging that damn guitar.'" After months of performing, he began to discover his true voice on the guitar, and people began to sit up and take notice.

In 1948, Montgomery was contracted by the Lionel Hampton Orchestra to perform on a national tour that took him throughout the United States. The hectic travel schedule, his commitment to his family and his fear of flying took their toll and led to his decision to leave the Hampton orchestra and return to Indianapolis. Back at home, Wes played at various clubs on Indiana Avenue to earn "pocket change," but in order to support his large family, his life became extraordinarily rigorous. He worked at the Polk's Milk Company from 7:00 a.m. to 3:00 p.m. and then played a gig at a bar from 9:00 p.m. to 2:00 a.m. Then he went to a club called the Missile Room and played there from 2:30 a.m. until 5:00 a.m. He also made his mark as a part of television history when he and his brothers Monk and Buddy backed up Flo Garvin on her jazz television program *Sentimental Journey*, which appeared on WFBM, channel 6, in 1951. It was the first jazz program starring a female singer.

Then lightning struck for Wes! On September 7, 1959, he hustled into Jacque Durham's Missile Room to perform a set. Jazz saxophonist Julian Cannonball

Adderley was in town for a concert and dropped by to hear Wes perform. Duncan Schiedt, music historian and organizer of the Indianapolis Jazz Club, was at the show and remembered the incident: "The set began, and before the first number was halfway through, Cannonball moved to a table directly in front of Montgomery, who was already showing his marvelous unique technique. The next memory I have is that Cannonball leaned way back in his chair, kind of slumped and rolled his eyes to the ceiling as if 'knocked out,' which he evidently was. He stayed rooted to his table all the time I was there."

The following morning, Cannonball telephoned Riverside Records producer Orrin Keepnews, who immediately signed Montgomery to a recording contract. Wes packed his bags for New York, where he

Wes Montgomery, considered by many the world's greatest jazz guitarist, topped the jazz polls for years but unfortunately died at an early age. His LPs are considered by jazz historians some of the best ever produced. *Courtesy of Duncan Schiedt.*

recorded his first album as a leader entitled *A Dynamic New Sound: The Wes Montgomery Trio*. His new recording contract propelled him to national celebrity status. Although the album received mixed reviews, it paved the way for his next album, *The Incredible Jazz Guitar of Wes Montgomery*, which received rave reviews and is considered one of his best works of art. That album earned him *Down Beat* magazine's New Star Award in 1960.

From this point onward, his popularity skyrocketed as jazz aficionados around the world were asking, "Who is this Wes Montgomery from some place called Naptown?" In 1965, Wes was nominated for two Grammy Awards for the album *Bumpin'*, and he received the Grammy Award for "Goin' Out of My Head" as best instrumental jazz performance in 1966. He was nominated for Grammy Awards again in 1968 for "Eleanor Rigby" and "Down Here on the Ground" and was nominated in 1969 for "Willow Weep for Me." In addition, he won *Down Beat* magazine's Critics Poll Award for best jazz guitarist in 1960, '61, '62, '63, '66 and '67. Jazz experts considered Wes Montgomery the greatest living jazz guitarist in the world. Sadly, he died at age forty-five of a heart attack on June 15, 1968, in Indianapolis.

One of Wes Montgomery's favorite sidemen was a gentleman who stood with Wes during their thin days as struggling musicians and carved out an important place for himself in the history of the Avenue. Thomas Edward Parker Jr. was born on August 12, 1929, to Evelyn Keys Parker and Thomas Edward Parker Sr. in Indianapolis. He received the nickname "Buddy" as a small child in honor of the family's beloved dog and carried it throughout the remainder of his life. He was one of twelve siblings, some of whom were musically gifted. Brothers Paul and Bobby respectively played the drums and the trumpet, and sister Mary sang. His father, Thomas Sr., taught each of his children the rudiments of music, played the saxophone himself and was well known in entertainment circles around the city. On many occasions, Parker Sr. appeared with various musical aggregations at the Sunset Terrace Ballroom on Indiana Avenue.

Parker attended Crispus Attucks High School, joined the band and began to study the saxophone under the supervision of Russell Brown. On many occasions, he was called to the front of the class to play, and Brown was always astonished by Parker's clarity and almost perfect pitch. Brown was a little skeptical of a student so young possessing this seemingly innate talent and investigated further. He discovered that Parker was playing almost perfectly "by ear" and not reading the music. He was one of the top music students in the band throughout his four years of high school.

After graduation, Parker grabbed his saxophone and hurried to Indiana Avenue in order to join the jazz music scene that was rapidly gaining notoriety. In 1949, he teamed up with the Montgomery brothers, with Wes on guitar, Monk on bass and Buddy on piano, and played nightly at the Ritz Nightclub. Later, a few doors down the Avenue, he performed with bassist Leroy Vinnegar and pianist Erroll "Ground Hog" Grandy at Henri's Nightclub. His longest tenure as a headliner occurred when he performed with Al Plank on piano, Al Kiger on trumpet, Benny Barth on drums and Andy Simpkins on bass at the Avenue's Comas Club. He also played on one of Wes Montgomery's earliest jazz albums.

In later years, Parker entered the world of politics and was convinced by civic leaders C. Keith Bulen and John Sweazy to join the Republican Party. He became active in local politics and was appointed director of the parking meter department. After his transition to politics, he largely withdrew from the entertainment scene, although he still performed with small groups at cultural events and private parties. Thomas Edward Parker Jr. died on April 18, 1990, in Indianapolis.

The influence of the magic of Wes Montgomery and his brothers was so overwhelming that it caused one young professional to pack his bags and move from Texas to Indiana. When he heard Wes playing guitar, a "bolt of lightning" struck his artistic soul, and Earl Theodore Dunbar "dropped his pharmacist spatula" and came running to Indiana Avenue. Dunbar was born on January 17, 1937, in Port Arthur, Texas. Both parents were pharmacists, so it was not surprising that his original vocational choice was in the field of pharmacy. His musical epiphany occurred in 1943 when his mother took him to a Duke Ellington concert. "Ever since that time, I could never forget that music; I could not get it out of my mind. Ever since that time, I've never stopped wanting to play jazz. I told her, 'If you wanted a pharmacist, you shouldn't have taken me to see Duke Ellington!'" He pleaded with his mother to purchase a trumpet, and after six months of study and practice, he garnered a spot in the Lincoln High School band.

"I had an excellent choral and band teacher in Oscar MacNeil, and I was influenced by Paul Richards of the Richards Brothers [David, Hal and Paul], who were the jazz musicians in town." Dunbar was able to graduate magna cum laude from the College of Pharmacy at Texas Southern University in Houston while jamming around town. He played with local musicians tenor saxophonists Arnett Cobb and Don Wilkerson, and after school, he worked as a pharmacist for his instructors in Houston. In 1958, during his last year in college, back stage at the Club Ebony, he met guitarist/flautist Les Spann, who played with Dizzy Gillespie's group. Les said, "Don't you play [the guitar] with your thumb? You ought to meet a guy named Wes Montgomery."

On a field trip to Indianapolis sponsored by his university, Dunbar quietly slipped across West Street to Jacque Durham's Missile Room. Slowly, he entered this smoke-filled, dimly lit cavern and noticed shadowy images moving on stage. He rubbed his eyes, then focused and saw and heard images and sounds that he had never experienced. There on the center stage, entertaining the jazz-crazed audience, were Wes Montgomery on guitar, Melvin Rhyne on organ and Paul Parker on drums. This experience further galvanized Dunbar's desire to put down the pill counter and pick up the guitar. "I went to the Missile Room nightly to hear Wes, Melvin and Paul. I had never heard anything like that in my life. It seemed like I was destined to be right there in that spot. When Wes finished playing, we got into his Mercury and we just talked and talked about the thumb thing and just everything. It was just what I was looking for, so I told my mother back in the drugstore, 'I'm sorry Ma, but I gotta go in my own direction,' and so I left there."

Dunbar telephoned his wife and advised her to pack up the furniture for the move to Indianapolis. Upon arriving, he worked as a pharmacist at Hooks Drug Store in the area of Indiana Avenue. Once settled in Indianapolis, he was influenced by Wes, Buddy and Monk Montgomery, bassist Larry Ridley and trombonist David Baker. "Baker was an intellectual genius who really helped me tremendously learning theory. Wes was like a raw flame genius. There was just music all the time...I played around Wes all the time. Never asked him questions about how you do something; we just played and it was beautiful."

In 1966, Dunbar went to New York and joined other performers in the city's jazz scene. His credits included stints with saxophonists Sam Rivers, Billy Harper and Frank Foster; pianists Kenny Barron and Gil Evans; and drummer Tony Williams. In 1972, bassist Larry Ridley, chairman of the Rutgers University/Livingston College music department in New Brunswick, New Jersey, began building the jazz performance degree program, and Dunbar was the second jazz professor whom he hired. Ridley's third hire in 1973 was Kenny Barron, who played with trumpeter Dizzy Gillespie in the 1960s and went on to become a professor of music at the Juilliard School of Music in New York. In 1975, Dunbar recorded the album *Kenny Barron & Ted Dunbar in Tandem* at a jazz concert in Lucy Stone Hall at Livingston College of Rutgers University. Subsequently, Ridley hired Frank Foster and drummer Freddie Waits. Ridley formed the Rutgers/Livingston

Jazz Professors, an ensemble that performed and conducted workshops in Phoenix, Arizona, and in Las Vegas, Nevada. The Vegas performances were organized by Fender bassist Monk Montgomery, who was then living there. Monk created the Las Vegas Jazz Society. He also arranged a booking of the Jazz Professors and himself to perform and do workshops in the country of Lesotho, sponsored by the Holiday Inns of Southern Africa.

Dunbar wrote several books, including *A System of Tonal Convergence for Improvisers, Composers and Arrangers* and *New Approaches to the Jazz Guitar.* One of his proudest teaching accomplishments was tutoring guitarist Kevin Eubanks, who later became the bandleader of the Jay Leno NBC television program *The Tonight Show.* Ted Dunbar died too young at age sixty-one, on May 29, 1998, in New Brunswick, New Jersey.

Among the young Turks baptized on the Avenue and who hooked up with the rising star of Wes Montgomery was keyboardist Melvin Rhyne. Historically, his claim to fame is that he was on stage at Jacque Durham's Missile Room when Cannonball Adderley discovered Montgomery in 1959. Melvin Russell Rhyne was born on October 12, 1936, to Aldrich Jacob Rhyne and Thelma Mitchell Rhyne in Indianapolis. He was raised in a working-class neighborhood on Rankin Street in proximity to Crispus Attucks High School. Melvin was first introduced to the world of music by his father, who was a self-taught piano player. His father's brother, George Rhyne, had moved out of his house, and Rhyne's family moved in; much to the delight of everyone, George left his piano. Rhyne's father would periodically pounce down on the piano stool and play some of the liveliest boogie-woogie tunes of the day. One day, as Melvin was totally mesmerized listening to his father's runs, he could not resist the temptation to play himself. He pleaded with his father to teach him the basic elements of boogie-woogie. His father agreed, sat young Rhyne down on the stool and began his boogie-woogie instruction.

Aside from the worldly pleasures of boogie-woogie, the Rhyne family often attended Mount Zion Baptist Church, where young Rhyne became entranced by the spiritually soothing, high-octane singing of the female quartets of his church. He was particularly impressed with the messages of hope and encouragement and the sincerity of their music. As he would sit, swaying and praying in his seat, he was able to appreciate the powerful spiritual impact of music. He nostalgically related about his early church experiences, "When we went to church, I listened especially to them sisters singing in there...If you had any kind of devil in you, when you leave there it's going to be gone."

Melvin Rhyne, sideman with Wes Montgomery, performed in Wisconsin for many years and cut many great CDs. *Courtesy of Melvin Rhyne Family Archives.*

As Rhyne polished his skill on the piano, he met a neighborhood friend, Lonnie Moore, who had a piano in his home and an equal passion for boogie-woogie music. Rhyne and Moore bonded in deep friendship and began to develop their musical skills by teaching each other new techniques that each had recently acquired. After months of practice, Rhyne and Moore had their neighborhood debut. One night, while practicing their music on Moore's front porch, they decided to set up a music platform at Smith and Missouri Streets. Accompanied by Rhyne's older brother Ronnie on drums, they held an impromptu boogie-woogie concert that could be heard throughout the neighborhood. When they looked up from their instruments toward the street, there were hundreds of fans clapping their hands and popping their fingers to the beat of their electrifying music.

On another memorable occasion, which occurred on a sunny Sunday afternoon, Rhyne and his father sat down at the piano and began to improvise some boogie-woogie tunes that had been popular on Indiana Avenue. As the church bells tolled and neatly dressed parishioners descended the church steps to return home, the sound of boogie-woogie music reverberated from the Rhyne house. The music was so spiritually uplifting and enticing that slowly, one by one, the parishioners climbed the Rhynes' stairs, entered through the screen door and formed a crowd in their front room. Amused but undaunted, Rhyne and his father increased their tempo to a higher intensity and got the crowd to shouting and singing. After the dust had settled, the parishioners realized that they had attended church for a religious service but had dropped by the Rhyne house and gotten a Sunday morning sermon. The Rhynes did not disappoint the flock.

Rhyne entered Crispus Attucks High School in 1950 and decided to continue his study of music. He met music teacher Russell Brown, who initially encouraged him to play the trombone because, as Brown explained, "You have some big chops." Rhyne experimented with the trombone for a while and played in the band and orchestra but returned to his first love, the piano, and joined a newly formed neighborhood jazz band called the Monarchs. It was composed of Melvin Rhyne on piano, James Spaulding on alto saxophone, Al Walton on tenor saxophone, David Hardiman on trumpet and Allen Moore on drums. The Monarchs were extremely popular among Indiana Avenue teenagers and would perform on weekends at the Walker Casino. Melvin later joined other Monarch band members and formed a group that backed rhythm-and-blues singer Percy Williams, who enjoyed success with his signature song, "Mercy Mr. Percy."

With Allen Moore on drums and John Lane on bass, Rhyne went to Indiana Avenue and performed nightly at Sea Ferguson's Cotton Club and George's Bar and traveled with trumpeter Elbert Cox, who performed with the Leo Hines and Dudley Storms Bands in the 1950s. Cox's slow, rhythmic walk and slow, silky-smooth and sophisticated diction earned him the moniker "Professor." He was the brother of Crispus Attucks High School science teacher Avalon Cox. Professor Cox booked gigs for them in Lafayette, where Rhyne earned sixty dollars per week. "In the 1950s, that was some pretty good ole spending change…I had every color of the Mr. B's dress shirt [a shirt with a collar that was round rather than lying flat, named in honor of popular jazz vocalist Billy Eckstein, who wore them when he performed], and I got my new record player too." As news of Rhyne's popularity began to circulate around Indiana Avenue, he was invited to perform with more seasoned and established musicians. Rhyne fondly remembered completing a final set in a club when a tall, willowy image slowly approached the bandstand. As he peered nervously through a cloud of dense cigarette smoke, he discovered that the image was a smiling Wes Montgomery. Montgomery was so impressed with his mastery on the keyboard that he invited him to join drummer Willis Kirk and himself at the Hub Bub Night Club, located on Thirtieth Street.

Rhyne switched from the piano to the Hammond B3 organ and accompanied Wes to Jacque Durham's Missile Room in 1959. During one late-night performance, nationally known saxophonist Cannonball Adderley strolled in to catch a set and was totally knocked out by the quality of the performance of Wes and his group. Rhyne was on the bandstand when Cannonball discovered Wes Montgomery. In 2011, Rhyne was still performing around town with the Melvin Rhyne Trio and the Rhyne Connection, featuring Frank Smith on bass and his sister, Carol Rhyne Harris, as vocalist. Melvin Rhyne died on March 5, 2013.

Another contemporary of Wes Montgomery who also captured the imagination of Indiana Avenue jazz patrons was Leslie William Taylor Jr. With his improvisational style and warm, cuddly demeanor, he came to be known as "Bear." Taylor was born in Indianapolis on August 9, 1931, to Leslie William Sr. and Harriet Marie Malone Taylor. In 1946, he entered Crispus Attucks High School and played saxophone in the band under the supervision of Russell Brown. After graduation from high school, he attended the Arthur Jordan Conservatory of Music at Butler University and later the Juilliard Conservatory of Music in New York. In 1951, he joined the United States Army and became a member of the Fourth Division Army Band in Germany. It was then that his army band mates bestowed on him the moniker "Bear Man" because of his burly physique and larger-than-life persona. While in Germany, he taught himself to play the flute, piano, trumpet, trombone, bass and alto sax.

Upon returning to Indianapolis after his army discharge, he began the serious and intense study of jazz under the tutelage of pianist Ground Hog Grandy. After months of rehearsing his scales and sharpening his skills on the finer aspects of music theory, Taylor got his first gig at Sea Ferguson's Cotton Club, where he sat in with guitarist Wes Montgomery, trombonist J.J. Johnson and bassist Larry Ridley. He also sat in with organist "Brother" Jack McDuff.

Les "Bear" Taylor, a great saxophonist who performed with Wes Montgomery on the bandstand and shared his talent with schoolkids in the classroom. *Courtesy of Carolyn Taylor-Carr.*

Taylor's daughter, Carolyn, fondly remembered as a young child the Sunday afternoon jam sessions at their home that included guitarist Wes, pianist Buddy, Fender bassist Monk Montgomery, drummer Paul Parker, trombonist Slide Hampton and guitarist James "Tiny" Adams. They would gather and play music all day. She remembered the warmth, camaraderie and fraternity that permeated their home as these musicians "strutted their best stuff" and delighted the neighbors with their snazzy jazz sounds.

Taylor began a recording career with some of the biggest names in show business. In 1956, he played baritone saxophone on both of organist/pianist Bill Doggett's rhythm-and-blues classics "Honky Tonk" and, three years later, "Hully Gully Twist." Taylor then recorded with rhythm-and-blues crooner Lloyd Price on two of his 1950s classic hits, "Stagger Lee" and "Personality." He traveled with the Bill Doggett Orchestra for ten years and later played with the Ella Fitzgerald Orchestra. In 1962, he recorded with vocalist Fitzgerald on her album entitled *Rhythm Is My Business* on the Verve label. That same year in New York, he recorded with vocalist Sarah Vaughan, trombonist Slide Hampton and drummer Charlie Persip. Persip was a member of Dizzy Gillespie's big band and became associate professor of jazz at the New School for Jazz and Contemporary Music in Manhattan (New York City). The following year, Taylor was the music director at the Baby Grand Jazz Club in Harlem and a member of the house band at the Apollo Theater.

Recognizing his years of experience in jazz and his knowledge of the recording industry, the Indianapolis Public School (IPS) system appointed him jazz artist-in-residence for four years. He was the executive producer and guest artist on an IPS music project album entitled *Jazz-o-Mania*. The album was accompanied by a booklet, co-authored with Patti Valentine, that featured jazz celebrities of Indianapolis. He was also responsible for developing prospective jazz students in the school system. Leslie William "Bear" Taylor Jr. died on November 15, 1983.

There were many great saxophonists to travel the entertainment circuit along Indiana Avenue in the early 1950s, and Alonzo Johnson was one of the best. Alonzo "Pookie" Johnson was born on October 5, 1927, to James Marion Dupee and Beatrice Fox in Indianapolis. His father, a tenor saxophonist/organist, lived in the neighborhood but did not play a significant role in Johnson's upbringing. On one very rare occasion, Johnson's dad presented him with a trumpet, an event not emblematic of their lifelong relationship. Shortly after receiving the gift, Johnson pushed the mouthpiece too far into the stem of the instrument and could not return it to its normal position. Exasperated, he took his newly acquired gift to a music store and presented it to the owner for repair. The owner immediately recognized the instrument as one purchased, but not fully paid for, by Dupee. "This is my instrument," the owner growled. "Your dad hasn't been back since he came in to put a down payment on it." The store owner took possession of the trumpet, and Johnson's career on that instrument, as well as any illusions about his father's generosity and goodwill, was dashed to bits.

Alonzo "Pookie" Johnson, considered by music historians one of the top three Avenue saxophonists of all time, also taught and mentored poor, inner-city youth. *Courtesy of Larry Goshen.*

Johnson attended Crispus Attucks High School, where, like many others, he acquired his music education under the tutelage of Russell Brown, LaVerne Newsome and Norman Merrifield. In 1945, Johnson enlisted in the United States Air Force and played in the Special Service Band, which traveled throughout the world entertaining troops. Returning to Indianapolis shortly after the war, Johnson joined several local bands and orchestras and spent several years touring the country. Although best known for his extraordinary gift as a jazz saxophonist, he mastered most wind instruments and could also play the piano. He appeared at many of the entertainment venues on Indiana Avenue, such as the Sunset Terrace, the Cotton Club, Henri's and the British Lounge. His recordings included *The Montgomery Brothers and Five Others, Together Again with Russell Webster, Say What* with Jimmy Coe and *Legacy,* which featured his sons Eric on piano, Byron on piano/trumpet and Kevin on vocals. Johnson also served as bandleader for the Wee Dots, the Pookie Johnson Quartet and the Indy Jazz Company. At various times, he performed with the Ink Spots, guitarist Wes Montgomery, bassists J.J. Johnson and Larry Ridley, trumpeter Freddie Hubbard, saxophonist James Moody and the Hampton sisters.

In addition to being a great saxophonist, Johnson made an enormous contribution to Indianapolis as a humanitarian who believed in giving back to the community. After retiring from employment at the post office for more than thirty years, he could have rested on his laurels and his celebrity and led a simple, carefree life. Instead, he made an investment in the youth of Indianapolis and found time to teach children about the joy of music. Mack Strong and his wife, vocalist Hazel Johnson-Strong, initiated a Saturday morning music program that partnered with the Indianapolis Jazz Foundation and the Indianapolis Public Schools. Gratuitously, he taught needy Indianapolis inner-city youth the rudiments of music and encouraged them to excel in their every academic endeavor. Johnson was one of Indiana Avenue's most beloved musicians. He died on September 3, 2005, in Indianapolis.

Another second-generation musician and jazz favorite following Pookie Johnson was Reginald Alfred DuValle Jr. DuValle had direct ancestral roots to the Walker Theatre and Indiana Avenue. He was the son of the acclaimed Reginald Alfred DuValle Sr., leader of the Blackbyrds Orchestra (which opened the Walker Theatre in 1927), and Oleatha Price DuValle. Reginald Jr. was born on April 27, 1927, in Indianapolis. From the time he was a tiny tot in the crib, young DuValle was constantly exposed to all genres of music. Musicians visited his home and practiced in his living room, and music students appeared at the doorstep to ask questions about the latest piano performing technique. The DuValle house was more than a wooden structure; it was a place where the musically inclined could come to obtain instruction and sharpen their skills.

In 1937, DuValle carried his trombone a few blocks in his neighborhood to the home of Crispus Attucks faculty member Norman Merrifield, where he received music lessons. As the years rolled by, DuValle attended Crispus Attucks High School, where his musical education continued with Russell Brown, Merrifield and LaVerne Newsome. His best friend, Russell Webster, recalled, "Me, Pookie and Reginald would sneak back into the music rooms at Attucks to broaden our musical horizons by experimenting with jazz, often sending the custodian into fits of frustration, trying to get us to stop when he was ready to go home."

In 1944, after graduation from high school, DuValle studied at the Indiana University School of Music with Newel Long. The following year, he was drafted into the United States Air Force, where he performed with the military band at Shepherd Field, Texas, and the United States 766th Air Force Band at Lockbourne, Ohio. In 1947, after leaving the service, he visited his sister Doris, who lived on 152nd Street in Harlem, New York City. He desperately wanted to hear the jazz bands in Greenwich Village, but since he did not know how to negotiate the New York subway, lugging his trombone under his arm, he walked several miles to Greenwich Village. On his way down Broadway, he turned a few corners and heard the lively beat of a jazz band coming through the doors of the Royal Roost Night Club. Cautiously, he entered the door.

To his surprise, his Indianapolis friend and legendary trombonist J.J. Johnson was rehearsing with bandleader Dizzy Gillespie for a show later that night. Johnson invited DuValle to sit. That was the day he got to play with the celebrated jazz great. While performing, he looked around the club and saw a patron passed out in his seat with his head on the table. That patron was trumpeter Charlie Parker.

DuValle earned his Bachelor of Music degree from Butler University's Jordan Conservatory of Music in 1950. During his tenure at Butler, he played with the college band, the Indianapolis Philharmonic Orchestra and several local jazz groups. DuValle's first

Reginald DuValle Jr., son of the bandleader who opened at the Walker Theatre in 1927. He performed with many local jazz groups and taught in the Indianapolis Public School system for many years. *Courtesy of Reginald DuValle Jr.*

job after graduation was at Florida A&M University, where he taught trombone, baritone saxophone, tuba, cello and the basics of conducting. He was also assistant band director for the marching, varsity and Reserve Officers' Training Corps (ROTC) bands. The university jazz band was led by alto saxophonist Julian "Cannonball" Adderley. When Cannonball left to pursue his recording career, DuValle filled his position. DuValle recalled that one of the tenor saxophone players in the band was Althea Gibson, who later became a world-famous Wimbledon tennis champion. DuValle said that she had so much air that he "almost never got her toned down enough to blend with the rest of the band." He also started an all-girl band because the university did not allow coeds to play with the marching band. In addition, he was a consultant with the Tallahassee School System.

Back in Indianapolis in 1953, DuValle began a thirty-seven-year career teaching music in the Indianapolis Public School system. In spite of the time constraints his teaching position presented, DuValle still found time to gig after hours with many of his friends who were considered the who's who in jazz on Indiana Avenue. In the hottest clubs on the Avenue, he performed with local jazz greats, including pianist Erroll Grandy, saxophonists Jimmy Coe and Buddy Parker, trumpeters Tommy Mullinex and Jim Edison, bassists Leroy Vinnegar and David Baker and drummer Paul Parker. He also gigged with national stars such as orchestra leaders Tiny Bradshaw and Lionel Hampton and vocalists Sammy Davis Jr., Marvin Gaye and Aretha Franklin.

In 1960, DuValle performed with the Larry Liggett Orchestra and produced a long-playing record entitled *Larry Liggett Swings at Stouffer's*. In the 1970s, he picked up his songwriter's quill, penned a song entitled "Where Are You Now?" and sent it to Hoagy Carmichael for his evaluation. A few months later, he received a tape in the mail of Carmichael performing the song on piano with Johnny Mercer as vocalist. DuValle closed out his career performing with Indianapolis's Brass Choir, Symphonic Band, the Concert Band and Brass Ensemble Society. He also played with the Steve Hayward Band. Reginald Alfred DuValle Jr. died on January 22, 2010.

Chapter 8

To Be or Not to Bop

Arguably, one of the most outstanding jazz scholars and professors of music in the world is an Indianapolis product born and bred, trained in the music department of Crispus Attucks High School. David Nathaniel Baker Jr. was born on December 21, 1931, to David Baker Sr. and Patress Baker. His earliest music instruction was received at Francis W. Parker School 56 under the supervision of Clara Kirk and Clarissa Winlock. He later attended John Hope School 26, where he studied under Dr. Roscoe Polin, who encouraged him to sing in the school choir. His earliest recollection of music with Polin was performing in the Christmas program. He clearly remembers singing "Angels We Have Heard on High."

In 1945, Baker entered Crispus Attucks High School, where he began instrumental music instruction under Russell Brown. His first choice of an instrument was the tuba, but unfortunately, the school did not have one in its inventory. Being an industrious and precocious student, Baker constructed a makeshift tuba from a cigar box and fishing string so that he could practice his fingering techniques. He came to class armed with his homemade contraption, played it and sang the tuba's music parts. Brown, recognizing Baker's determination, obtained a sousaphone and presented it to his creative student.

In the 1940s, a new music genre was born: bebop. Jazz pioneers such as Charlie Parker on alto saxophone, Dizzy Gillespie on trumpet, Thelonious Monk and Bud Powell on piano, Clifford Brown on trumpet and Coleman Hawkins on tenor saxophone were innovators in this new art form, which

David Baker, one of the premier jazz educators in the world, also distinguished himself by performing with great groups, such as the George Russell Sextet. *Courtesy of David Baker.*

swept the nation. Being a progressive music educator, Brown quickly recognized the dynamism of this new art form and incorporated it into his lesson plans. He organized a jazz band composed of the brightest music students in the department and christened them the Rhythm Rockets. The musicians in the group, with occasional personnel changes on the different instruments, included Earmon Hubbard and Trili Yvonne Stuart on piano, David Young and George Bright on tenor saxophone and Tillman Buggs and David Baker on trombone. Brown gave his students additional instruction in music theory and literacy with an emphasis on improvisation. Baker remembered Brown exhorting his students to stand up and "testify" during a song. The term "testify" was a code word for improvisation, and students were able to play their instruments freely and not be concerned with time-honored rules and convention.

After school, Baker would sit attentively by his old, trusty Arvin radio and listen to the latest songs on the *Easy Gwen* radio program on the WIBC radio station. He listened and sang along with the popular hits of the day. On Sundays, he sang in the choir at Eastern Star Baptist Church and would spend the entire day in service. He remembered seeing famous traveling quartets of the day, such as the Chicago-based Soul Stirrers, featuring a youthful Sam Cooke, who later transitioned to popular music and recorded "You Send Me," the rhythm-and-blues classic that topped the music charts in December 1957. Baker was overwhelmed by their harmony and showmanship when they came to his church and performed the latest gospel songs.

The preparation that Baker received under the tutelage of Russell Brown prepared him to venture into Indianapolis's night life and test his chops. He had transitioned from the tuba to the trombone and was anxious to "test the water." Among his first engagements were performances at the 16th Street Tavern and at the 19th Hole with either Tiny Adams or Mingo Jones on bass, Earl Van Riper on piano and Robert "Sonny" Johnson on drums. Later, he traveled to California and joined the Stan Kenton Orchestra—he and Curtis Counce became its first African American band members.

In 1949, Baker entered the Arthur Jordan Conservatory of Music and studied the baritone horn for one year. His tenure at the conservatory was short-lived when he was dismissed from school for dancing with a white girl at a Christmas party. In 1950, he entered Indiana University intending to study to become a classical trombonist, but he encountered numerous racism-based obstacles with which he had to contend. African Americans were not allowed to live on campus, could not be served in restaurants and hotels in downtown Bloomington and were viewed as second-class citizens. On one occasion, while traveling with the Indiana University Orchestra and choir to a concert at Carnegie Hall in New York, the bus stopped at a restaurant. Baker, the only African American student among 150 people, was refused service; however, the conductor, Dr. Ernst Hoffman, said, "If you're not going to serve him, you're not going to serve anybody." Immediately, all members of the group left the restaurant to seek another place to eat. While in school, Baker organized a jazz orchestra that was composed of former university students and Indiana Avenue musicians. He majored in music education and received a bachelor's degree in 1952 and a master's in 1954.

In 1959, Gunther Schuller of the Metropolitan Opera Orchestra of New York witnessed a performance of Baker's orchestra in Bloomington and offered him a scholarship to study at the Lenox School of Jazz in Lenox, Massachusetts. Baker has studied with a wide range of master teachers, performers and composers, including trombonist J.J. Johnson, cellist Janos Starker and pianist and composer George Russell. He is an award-winning performer/composer/educator who was nominated for a Pulitzer Prize in 1973 and a Grammy in 1979 and won an Emmy in 2003. He has performed and taught all around the world.

The name Count Fisher became synonymous with the jazz trio concept that was very popular on the Avenue in the 1950s. Fisher, a drummer, introduced Aretta La Marre, singer, and Chuck Bush and Charles Cox, both tenor saxophonists, to the Indiana Avenue jazz scene. They were among the first black performers to play the Comas Club. Lessly "Count" Fisher

Count Fisher, a jazz musician who performed in many of the clubs on and off Indiana Avenue.

was born on August 19, 1923, to Seaser Fisher and Ruby Mosby Fisher in Canton, Mississippi. Seeking better economic opportunities, the family moved from Mississippi to Gary and later to East Chicago, Indiana, where his father sought employment in the steel mills. Fisher attended the local public schools and graduated from George Washington High School in 1941. He followed in his father's footsteps and went to work in the steel mills, but due to an industrial accident, he changed careers, entering the world of music. He joined his cousin's band the Night Steppers, playing the drums. Fisher, along with his childhood friend, jazz organist Jack McDuff, was taught to read music by local musician Jesse Evans.

In 1951, Fisher met vocalist Eve Renee in Indianapolis, and they performed at the Hub Bub Night Club and the Joy Lounge. They eventually married and established the Carousel Club in Indianapolis in the late 1950s. The club featured such performers as tenor saxophonist John Coltrane, jazz organists Jimmy McGriff and Jack McDuff, bassist Leroy Vinnegar, trumpeter Freddie Hubbard, rhythm-and-blues artist James Brown and comedians Rodney Dangerfield, Redd Foxx, George Kirby and Moms Mabley. They established another club in Indianapolis, the Chateau de Count, where they showcased vocalists Roy Hamilton and Lula Reed, and the Motown Review, which showcased performers from the Detroit-based record company. In 1966, Fisher and Renee relocated to Grand Rapids, Michigan, where they worked as the house band at the London House. After they retired from performing, they remained in Grand Rapids.

Several Indiana Avenue performers were schooled on the finer points of jazz at the Hampton home, 529–31 Vermont Street, just a few blocks south of Indiana Avenue. After jamming in their basement, they later performed with various Hampton family members and others during the late 1940s and throughout the 1950s. William Penick, one of the students from the "Hampton school," son of Walter Sr. and Nellie Penick, was born on January 4, 1932, in Indianapolis. As a youngster, he listened to saxophonist Illinois Jacquet and bandleader/clarinetist Benny Goodman on the radio and often fantasized about having a successful career in the world of music. He attended Mary E. Cable School 4 and sang in the choir and then went on to Crispus Attucks High School, where he met Russell Brown and joined the school band. "Mr. Brown was the greatest; he taught me my first notes on the saxophone. All the kids loved him, and he was a father figure to the kids," he related. Penick also sang in the boys' choir, directed by Norman Merrifield, whom he considered "very dedicated but strict."

After high school, Penick studied at the McArthur Conservatory of Music for two years. His first entertainment break came when he joined the Hampton Family Band and performed at Stein's Jazz Club on Meridian Street. In 1951, he entered the United States Army Special Service Unit and played in the military band. On one occasion, his band backed up comedian Bob Hope on one of his tours with the United Service Organization (USO). After being discharged from the service, Penick returned to Indianapolis and played in a combo with trombonist Slide Hampton and trumpeter Maceo Hampton at the Harem Jazz Club. Intermittently, he performed with bandleaders Lavon Kemp, Larry Liggett and the Eldridge Morrison Orchestra. Penick was still performing as a solo act or with various jazz groups around the city in 2011.

Al Coleman's Three Souls was formed in 1969 when Coleman purchased the British Lounge, located at 643 Indiana Avenue. The members were Coleman on drums, Clarence McCloud on piano and

Bill Penick, a saxophonist who cut his chops with the Hampton Family Band and performed with many groups on Indiana Avenue. He learned his trade jamming at the Hampton home in the mid-1940s. *Courtesy of Mark Sheldon.*

Eugene Fowlkes on bass. Subsequently, there were two personnel changes on bass as Louis "Tiny" Adams replaced Fowlkes and later Carl Bailey replaced Adams. Adams was morbidly obese, weighing more than six hundred pounds, and died when he was still a young man. The man who replaced Adams, Carl Wilbur Bailey Sr., was born on June 9, 1918, to Thomas Edward and Mary Callie Olden Bailey in Indianapolis. During World War II, he served in the United States Army and played with the USO band. He declined an offer to tour with the Count Basie Orchestra and also performed as a guitarist with the Hampton Family Band. In 1973, Al Coleman's Three Souls, with Bailey on bass, recorded "Herbie's Tune" for the All-Indy Record Company. Bailey died on July 12, 1986, in Indianapolis.

In 1952, when Jimmy Coe's Orchestra performed at the Cotton Club in Cincinnati, the baritone saxophone player with Coe was Bill Boyd. William Calvan Boyd Jr. was born on March 8, 1931, to William Sr. and Ardelia Louise Leavell Boyd in Indianapolis. His earliest music instruction was received at George Washington Carver School 87, where he studied under Ruth McArthur and James Compton. He entered Crispus Attucks High School in 1940, joined the orchestra and band and studied with Russell Brown, Norman Merrifield and LaVerne Newsome. At Crispus Attucks, some of his music contemporaries were Tillman Buggs and David Baker on trombone and Les Bear Taylor on baritone saxophone. In the late 1940s, he performed on Indiana Avenue with many notable jazz aggregations, among them Dudley Storms, Eldridge Morrison, Lavon

Kemp, Larry Liggett and saxophonist David Young. In the early 1950s, he toured with Jimmy Coe's Orchestra throughout the Midwest. Bill Boyd died on October 27, 2002, in Indianapolis.

Jazz being an art form associated with intellectualism and culture compelled one individual to seek instruction outside his genre in order to explore newer dimensions in music. Eugene Fowlkes, who like Carl Bailey performed with Jimmy Coe, began his career on the trombone and later opted for the bass. Fowlkes was not content with being just another musician. He wanted to be the best he could possibly be and raise his performance level to that of his jazz contemporaries on the Avenue, some of whom had received international acclaim. Therefore, later in his music career, he sought classical music instruction from Herbie Guy, the principal bassist of the Indianapolis Symphony Orchestra.

Eugene Augustus Fowlkes was born on February 7, 1930, to Marshall Fowlkes and Elizabeth Trotter Fowlkes in Indianapolis, Indiana. He attended Crispus Attucks High School, where he studied the trombone with Russell Brown, but he completed his education in the United States Army in 1947. After military service, he enrolled in the McArthur Conservatory of Music, studied the trombone with Slide Hampton and performed with the Hampton Family Band under the direction of Duke Hampton in 1953. His jazz debut on Indiana Avenue took place at Henri's Nightclub and was highlighted by his performance with some of Indianapolis's up-and-coming jazz artists. He shared the bandstand with luminaries such as Wes Montgomery on guitar, Monk Montgomery on bass, Carl Perkins on piano and Carroll Engs on drums.

In 1954, Fowlkes hit the road with Jimmy Coe's Orchestra and toured many southern states where the policy of segregation was strictly enforced. Being a proud individual, he refused to abide by local laws and insisted on drinking from whites-only drinking fountains. On several occasions, the orchestra members were nearly run out of town because of his rebellious attitude toward segregation. In the mid-1950s, as performance gigs with the trombone began to fade, Fowlkes switched to the bass to obtain more work. One wet and windy Friday night, he journeyed down Indiana Avenue to Sack's Pawn Shop and purchased a bass. He was determined to master the instrument so that his skills would be more marketable in the jazz community. He taught himself basic fingering techniques, and when his instruction required more theory, he received instruction from bassists Phillip "Flip" Stewart and Monk Montgomery.

In the 1960s, Fowlkes performed with bandleader Lenny Wilson and his orchestra, who worked hotels, nightclubs and music festivals throughout the state. Shortly thereafter, tragedy struck. Fowlkes was seriously injured as the result of a fall that left him paralyzed from his waist down. He was informed by medical personnel that he would never walk again, but his fierce determination and commitment that had refused to yield to Jim Crow laws in the South came to the fore. He was determined to walk again, and he did. Word of Fowlkes's misfortune circulated in the jazz fraternity, and because other musicians respected his technical precision on the bass, they came to his aid. Lenny Wilson, who had been contracted to perform at Holiday Inn hotels throughout Indiana, in a display of respect and admiration, held fundraisers for Fowlkes to defray a portion of his medical expenses. Fowlkes resumed his career as bassist and was the only African American in Lenny Wilson's orchestra.

As his star continued to rise, Fowlkes performed at some of the hottest jazz clubs on and surrounding Indiana Avenue, such as the Cotton Club, Trianon Ballroom, Flamingo Club, Walker Casino, Hub Bub, Mr. B's, Topper, 19th Hole and Cactus Club. His services were in high demand. In the 1960s, he performed with the Claude Sifferin Trio, with Sifferin on piano and Jack Ireland on drums, and also with the Three Souls, which featured Al Coleman on drums, Clarence McCloud on piano and Fowlkes on bass.

Fowlkes's artistic ability became such a hot commodity that pianist/bandleader Earl "Fatha" Hines dispatched his manager to Indianapolis to recruit Fowlkes. Fowlkes agreed and toured with Hines for more than two years throughout the United States. One of his fondest memories was being surprised by his beloved little sister, Betty, when she casually strolled into the Village Gate during his performance and shocked him. Fowlkes died on February 25, 2005.

In the 1940s and 1950s, the *Indianapolis Recorder* kept its readers aware of the jazz scene on Indiana Avenue. One drummer who also doubled as the *Recorder* music editor was Bob Womack. Robert Womack was born on July 1, 1916, in Jackson, Tennessee, to Bessie B. and Arthur Walter Womack. As a youngster in the backwoods of western Tennessee, he was exposed to the guttural blues howling of Robert Johnson, Son House and Howling Wolf. He later performed with some of the greatest jazz performers who came through town. On the local scene, he performed with orchestra leaders Jimmy Coe, Dudley Storms, Arthur VanDyke and Eldridge Morrison. At the *Recorder*, for many years, Womack wrote the column "Believe Me When I Tell You." Bob Womack died on December 23, 1984, in Indianapolis.

From 1966 until 1983, Lavon Kemp was mentioned twelve times in Bob Womack's "Believe Me When I Tell You" and "Know Your Entertainers" columns in the *Indianapolis Recorder*. Lavon Anthony Kemp was a musician from an earlier generation of big-band music and was not really proficient as a jazz performer; however, many of the younger musicians rallied around him, performed with him, modernized his art form and made it more appealing to the Indiana Avenue jazz community. Kemp was born on May 4, 1914, in Indianapolis and received his early musical instruction under Harold Brown at Crispus Attucks High School. Kemp served in the United States Navy for two years and performed with the seventeen-piece Navy Orchestra. After his discharge from military service, he returned to Indianapolis, where he organized the Lavon Kemp Orchestra, which was extremely popular in the nightclubs of Indiana Avenue. Lavon Kemp died on August 8, 2003, in Indianapolis.

A young jazz student who graduated from the ranks of the Lavon Kemp Orchestra and was instrumental in modernizing Kemp's repertoire by influencing Kemp to play more contemporary standards was drummer Ray Cumberland. Cumberland was born on October 21, 1934, to Dorothy Cumberland in Cincinnati, Ohio. As a youngster, he spent countless hours at the neighborhood Regal Theatre watching the popular Hollywood movies roll across the silver screen. As an added attraction, the theater presented internationally and nationally known personalities to entertain the patrons during intermissions. Cumberland vividly remembered seeing stars such as orchestra leaders Duke Ellington, Count Basie and Lionel Hampton; vibraphonist Milt Jackson; vocalist Ella Fitzgerald; and comedian George Kirby, "the man with a million voices."

Cumberland remembered that he was encouraged to play trumpet after seeing the movie *Man with a Horn*, which starred Kirk Douglas. In 1940, the Cumberland family moved to Indianapolis, where he attended Public School 23. There he took trumpet lessons from Larry Liggett. Cumberland later met a former Indiana Avenue singer, Bertha Eubanks, who taught him to play the drums. Her son, Donald, was the leader and vocalist of the Eubanks Quintet, and this was Cumberland's first performance experience.

Cumberland attended Crispus Attucks High School and further developed his musical skills under the baton of Russell Brown. He comically recalled that during his music class, while Brown was absent from the classroom, he and his classmate Al Walton, along with other students, would strike up an impromptu jam session and play many of the latest jazz tunes rather than the songs required by Brown. "While the students were jamming, there was one student at the door who served as a lookout and would holler, 'He yaw, Mr. Brown is coming!' Immediately, the students would stop jamming and return to their music lessons."

Cumberland practiced with the Hampton Family Band and received superb musical instruction from the family patriarch, Deacon Hampton. He nostalgically remembered the finer entertainment pointers that he received from this experience and further instruction he got from orchestra leaders Dudley Storms and Eldridge Morrison. "The main thing was keeping time; they don't care how great you were, but when we played those dances, the man said keep that beat…don't lose the beat," he recounted.

In the early 1950s, he performed with stars such as Dudley Storms, the Al Walton Trio, Willis Dyer, Lavon Kemp's big band, Wes Montgomery, Jimmy Coe and the Eldridge Morrison big band. He also performed with Indiana Avenue entertainers such as bandleader Jimmy McDaniels and vocalists Flo Garvin and Ophelia Hoy. In addition to being a widely sought drummer, Cumberland displayed another dimension of his artistic ability by assuming the role of a vocalist. His signature songs were "I Don't Know Why I Love You Like I Do," "That Old Black Magic" and many of Billy Eckstein's signature songs. In 2011, Cumberland was still performing around Indianapolis with the Carl Hines Trio, the Jack Brink Orchestra and the Harry Maginity Conversion Band. Does "still performing" sound like he'll never stop?

Yet another Crispus Attucks music student, a contemporary of Cumberland who was the pride and joy of Russell Brown, was tenor saxophonist David Young. David Young was born on October 23, 1933, to Flora Elliot Young and David Elmire Young in Indianapolis. An only child, he graduated from Crispus Attucks High School and attended Butler University, Indiana University and Kentucky State College. He served in the United States Army, where he played in the band at Fort Knox, Kentucky, and Frankfort, Germany. He played professionally with the Duke Ellington Orchestra, the George Russell Sextet, the Lionel Hampton Orchestra, the Frank Foster Big Band, the Jack McDuff Quintet, Nigerian drummer Michael Olatunji and His Drums of Passion and Sam River's Harlem Ensemble. Cited for his lifetime pursuit of excellence in music, he received the key to the city and investiture in the Congressional Record as a jazz legend by United States senator Richard Lugar. Also, he was featured on the Jazz Greats Hall of Fame mural at the Watkins Family Life Center. He recorded his widely acclaimed first album entitled *David Young* with jazz greats Virgil Jones on trumpet, Sonny Fortune on alto/tenor saxophone, Richard Davis on bass, Harold Mabern Jr. on piano and Idris Muhammad on drums. He died on February 6, 2009, in Indianapolis, Indiana.

David Young, a saxophonist who joined David Baker with the George Russell Sextet, is considered to be among the top three best saxophonists to ever grace Indiana Avenue. *Courtesy of Larry Goshen.*

Being the offspring of the First Family of Indiana Avenue jazz was a rough row to hoe. Paulea Kerley Rhyne, later known as Paula Hampton, was born on July 11, 1938, to Paul Kerley and Aletra Hampton-Kerley of the Hampton sisters. This group was composed of Hampton's aunts Virtue, Carmalita and Dawn. As a young child, she was totally immersed in the world of music, as her relatives were professional musicians well regarded in the entertainment community. Entrepreneurially inclined as a child, she comically remembered constructing small bleachers with cinder blocks and wooden planks and charging an admission fee so that neighborhood children could hear her relatives rehearse. Also, Hampton fondly remembered sitting in her living room and witnessing her uncle Slide Hampton rehearsing on his trombone for hours. She desperately wanted to emulate her uncle but regretfully recalled, "My arms were too short, and I couldn't reach the seventh position."

In 1951, she entered Crispus Attucks High School and studied music with Russell Brown. Concerning Brown, she recalled, "He was an outstanding music educator who encouraged each student to strive toward excellence to be the best. Time didn't matter to him. He'd spend all day going over musical charts to make sure you'd understand them well. He was the best."

Hampton's maiden introduction to the performance component of jazz oddly occurred on the bandstand of her uncle Duke Hampton. One night, preparing to perform at Sea Ferguson's Cotton Club, Duke realized that his drummer would miss the gig due to the debilitating effects of the spirits of alcohol. He needed a replacement drummer immediately. Nervously, he approached Paula and convinced her to temporarily replace the drummer, telling her, "Sit down here and keep the beat until I find somebody to take your place." From this musical experience onward, Paula developed a love for playing the drums.

In the mid-1950s, Hampton performed with various jazz aggregations at the top jazz spots along Indiana Avenue, including the Sunset Terrace Ballroom, George's Bar, the Place to Play and Tuffy Mitchell's establishments. In 1962, she relocated to New York City and continued performing. For seven years, she backed jazz vocalist Dakota Staton and headed her own jazz aggregation, the Jazzberry Jam, which was a favorite among jazz aficionados.

Chapter 9

Jazz Marches On

M any Indiana Avenue stars gained formidable exposure by performing in plush supper clubs with neatly attired doormen, valet parking and the glitz and glamour of Meridian Street and at private parties in the suburbs, but they still maintained their common touch. Most still regarded Indiana Avenue as home base and reserved their finest performances for adoring jazz aficionados in the clubs that lined its corridor. One such star was James Andrew "Jimmy" McDaniels. He was born on January 23, 1929, in Vinesville, Alabama, the second son of Charles Andrew McDaniels and Willie Viola Selden-McDaniels. In 1918, his father attended Tuskegee Institute in Tuskegee, Alabama, and his mother was the first woman to graduate from Miles College in Fairfield, Alabama. Both parents taught piano and the woodwind instruments at Fairfield Industrial High School and Miles College.

His father, a music professor, encouraged his children to play instruments, and four sons—James, Charles, Leroy and Braxton—followed in their father's footsteps and excelled in music. James played piano/alto saxophone, Charles played piano/soprano saxophone, Leroy played piano/baritone saxophone and Braxton played piano/alto saxophone. During the Christmas season, all of the sons paraded around the house and serenaded their parents with Yuletide songs.

McDaniels graduated from Fairfield Industrial High School in 1947 and attended Miles College from 1947 until 1949. Because of the intolerable racial climate in Alabama, McDaniels moved to Toledo, Ohio, and attended the Toledo Conservatory of Music in 1953. Later, he moved to Grand Rapids, Michigan, and then to Indianapolis and took graduate courses in music and psychology at Indiana University in the late 1940s. From 1949 until 1953, he served as a paratrooper and bandleader with the Eighty-second Airborne Division while stationed at Fort Bragg in Fayetteville, North Carolina.

In 1965, McDaniels received the Governor's Award for outstanding service to Indiana for his organization of a jazz band at the Pendleton Reformatory. In the 1970s, he was an education specialist, soloist and guest conductor with the Indianapolis Symphony Orchestra during the tenure of music directors Izler Solomon and John Nelson. McDaniels taught a music course entitled "Roots of African-American Jazz" at Indiana University–Purdue University at Indianapolis (IUPUI) in 1981.

His daughter Marla McDaniels-Heath received a Bachelor of Music degree in 1976 from the Indiana University School of Music and has performed on opera stages throughout the country. His cousin Eugene McDaniels was an accomplished songwriter and for many years was the principal songwriter for popular music singer Roberta Flack. Jimmy McDaniels died on April 25, 2009.

While Jimmy McDaniels performed at nightclubs in the suburbs, taught music at Indiana University–Purdue University at Indianapolis and guest conducted the Indianapolis Symphony Orchestra, only a few blocks east, there was a husband-and-wife jazz duo that performed in many of the night spots on Indiana Avenue. Charles Leonard "Chuck" Bush was born on June 26, 1925, to Tecumseh Baines and Esther Marie White Bush in Peoria, Illinois. He received his early music education in the public school system and left the city at nineteen to join the circus. He fondly recalled living across the street from future Hollywood movie star and comedian Richard Pryor, and on many occasions, he baby-sat Pryor. Bush played with a local band at many venues in towns in the neighboring states of Indiana, Ohio and Kentucky.

Arriving in Indianapolis in the early 1950s, he joined the Count Fisher Trio, which included Fisher on drums, Erroll Grandy on piano and Bush on tenor saxophone. They appeared at the major venues on Indiana Avenue such as the Sunset Terrace Ballroom, Cotton Club, George's Bar and Orchid Room and the Place to Play. Staying in Indianapolis but leaving Indiana Avenue, he played at the Hub Bub and the 19th Hole. He comically remembered performing at the 19th Hole with the female impersonator "Miss Tangy Dupree." According to Bush, Miss Dupree, dressed in a skintight body suit, seductively and exotically danced around the club with an eight-foot boa constrictor snake wrapped around his neck. Bush remembered nervously playing his saxophone while the snake took its tour of the club. For many years, Bush backed up his wife, Aretta La Marre. Charles Leonard Bush died on April 21, 1980.

Aretta Doretha Thomas La Marre Bush was born on August 9, 1930, to Arthur and Sarah Lee Thomas in East Chicago, Indiana. During her early childhood, she developed an intense love for music as she serenaded and was serenaded by her father as she played around the house. She sang in the choirs at Franklin Elementary School, Washington High School and her church and found great delight in entertaining others. In 1948, she moved to New York, where she performed with legendary entertainers, including vocalists Sarah Vaughan, Billie Holiday, Dinah Washington and Ella Fitzgerald. She was also a vocalist with the Duke Ellington Orchestra. For a short period, she roomed with vocalist Billie Holiday, and both appeared at Carnegie Hall, where Aretta sang "Danny Boy" and won first place in a talent competition.

In the early 1950s, she moved to Indianapolis and was the headliner at the Ferguson Hotel with Jimmy Coe's Orchestra. She appeared at nightclubs throughout the city, such as the 19th Hole, Pink Poodle and Al Coleman's British Lounge.

Chuck Bush, a saxophonist who baby-sat comedian Richard Pryor in Peoria, Illinois. *Courtesy of Linda Bush.*

Aretta La Marre, wife of Chuck Bush, performed with the Count Fisher Trio. She once bested singer Billie Holiday in a contest in New York. *Courtesy of Linda Bush.*

She recorded the song "You Won't Be Seeing Me," accompanied by Al Coleman's Three Souls, on the All Indy record label. Years later, she returned to gospel music and performed with the Lavelle Inspirational Singers, the Gospel Pearls, the Blakely Specials, Al Hobbs and Eternal Light and the Gospel Music Workshop of America. She reentered the recording studio with the Gospel Pearls and recorded the songs "Lead Me On" and "Just Tell Jesus" on the Soul Music Company label. She died on June 26, 2006, in Indianapolis.

Contemporaries of Chuck Bush and Aretta La Marre were two brothers who performed in the clubs on Indiana Avenue. Richard Lee Laswell was born on March 1, 1931, to Merrill Walter Laswell Sr. and Lorena Coleman Laswell in Indianapolis. He was the youngest of three sons. When he was only sixteen months old, his father was killed, and this left his mother with four mouths to feed. With minimal education in a rough post–Great Depression economy, his mother was determined to raise her family. She sought employment as a domestic worker and took in laundry to earn additional money to make ends meet. Realizing the difficult economic obstacles with which his mother had to contend, Laswell sought employment after school to help his mother financially. He established a shoeshine service business in which he traveled throughout the neighborhood collecting shoes in his tiny red wagon. He took the shoes home, shined them and returned them to his customers the same day. He earned twenty-five cents per pair of shoes and was proud to give it to his mother.

When Laswell became a teenager, he developed a fascination with all types of music. He often visited the home of his cousin, Albert Coleman, and his uncle, Alvia Coleman, who was a drummer with the popular Brown Buddies group. Quietly, sitting on the front porch and peering through a large screen door, Laswell was mesmerized by the intricate rhythmic patterns that his uncle played with his sticks on the drum skin. His uncle noticed the inquisitive lad on the porch and later took him under his wing, teaching him the rudiments of percussion instruments.

After the music lessons with his uncle, Laswell attended Francis Bellamy School 37 and John Hope School 26 and received instruction from Ruth McArthur. In 1945, he entered Crispus Attucks High School to study the percussion instruments under Russell Brown, became the drum major in the marching band and played in the orchestra directed by LaVerne Newsome.

While in high school, Laswell wanted to expand his musical horizon, so he convinced his brother Merrill to permit him to play the drums in his orchestra. He was underage and needed a plan to remedy the situation. He consulted his mother and asked for permission to perform at the Savoy Night Club. She gave him a note to deliver to the club owner that gave him permission to be in the club.

Laswell graduated from high school in 1949 and joined the United States Marine Corps the following year. He auditioned and won a seat in the service band at Camp Lejeune, North Carolina, and performed with the aggregation at many military bases around the world.

After his discharge from the military, Laswell returned to Indianapolis and played in many of the jazz clubs around the city. He appeared with various musical groups at the Sunset Terrace, George's Orchid Room, the Cotton Club and Henri's Nightclub. Later, he teamed up with blues vocalist Ophelia Hoy and performed at the Brass Rail for five years. He led the Dickie Laswell Trio at the Jazz Cooker and remained there for fifteen years. Laswell died on April 14, 2002.

Laswell's older brother, Merrill, was a drummer who performed on Indiana Avenue. Merrill Walter Laswell Jr. was born on March 15, 1922, in Indianapolis. He attended Crispus Attucks High School and studied music under the supervision of Norman Merrifield. During World War II, he joined the U.S. Army Air Corps and its Special Service unit as a trombonist in its military band. After the war, returning to Indianapolis, Laswell furthered his music education by studying at the McArthur Conservatory of Music on Indiana Avenue.

In his weekly entertainment column in the *Indianapolis Recorder*, Bob Womack paid a special tribute to his dear friend:

> *The entire local and national musical fraternity was shaken by the death last week of Merrill Walter Laswell, Jr. prominent jazz trumpeter, composer, arranger and bandleader. He was also known as a great humanitarian among musicians and laymen alike. Laswell was taught to play the trumpet by his uncle Hugh T. Taylor, a trombonist and professional musician... starting in the 1940s, he played with many local and nationally known bands over the country namely Bob Womack and the Twelve Bobcats as player and road manager. He also performed with the orchestras and bands of Clarence Love, Tiny Bradshaw, Dudley Storm, Lavon Kemp, Wheeler Moran, Snookum Russell, Frank Reynolds, Eldridge Morrison and with the Jimmy Coe large inter-racial orchestra as a guest artist. In between time when he was not wailing with other aggregations, my old buddy was fronting his own all-star combo. He was instrumental in helping many cats up the ladder of musical success including the late Earl "Fox" Walker and*

Willis Kirk, drummers respectively, J.J. Johnson, a top trombonist on the international scene and the one and only Wes Montgomery, guitarist.

Laswell died on August 8, 1973.

From the late 1940s and throughout the 1950s, Bob Womack was the entertainment editor for the *Indianapolis Recorder* with his column "Believe Me When I Tell You." In addition to being a journalist, Womack, a drummer, was a frequent entertainer in many of the jazz spots on Indiana Avenue. His group, Bob Womack and His Bobcats, regularly featured Merrill Laswell on drums. From the Down Beat nightclub near Tenth Street to George's Bar near Michigan Street, Bob Womack's crew packed late-night revelers in the house and was considered the "Toast of the Town," according to the jazz aficionados who frequented the clubs. Who was this Bob Womack?

Robert Womack was born on July 1, 1916, in Jackson, Tennessee, to Arthur Walter and Bessie B. Womack. As a youngster, he heard the blues booming out the doors of speakeasies and juke joints ninety miles northeast of Memphis. After moving to Indianapolis, Womack attended Crispus Attucks High School and became a star player on the football team. While not practicing on the gridiron, he became an excellent music student under the supervision of Norman Merrifield and LaVerne Newsome and was a member of both the band and orchestra. After graduation, he journeyed to Indiana Avenue, where his musical ability was immediately recognized, and performed with nationally and internationally known jazz performers who traveled through town. Entertainers such as bandleaders Tiny Bradshaw, Lionel Hampton, Frank Reynolds and Lucky Millinder and trumpeter Dizzy Gillespie often sought the services of Womack. On the local scene, he performed with the orchestras and bands of Jimmy Coe, Dudley Storms, Arthur VanDyke and Eldridge Morrison. Bob Womack died on December 23, 1984, in Indianapolis.

Womack chronicled many jazz entertainers from Indianapolis in his *Recorder* column and was mindful of the fact that out-of-towners contributed to its proud entertainment legacy. The State of Missouri has always proudly boasted its identifiable sobriquet as the "Show Me State," which denoted hard work, stubbornness and perseverance. In the middle of the twentieth century, two Missourians traveled to Indiana, transplanted themselves and entertained many of the jazz lovers on Indiana Avenue. Floyd George Broomfield Smith was born on January 25, 1917, in St. Louis to William Amerald Smith and Mary Jane Smith and was the youngest son of nine children. His father was a railroad man who tinkered on the snare drums in his spare time, and his mother was a housewife. When Smith was ten years old, a family friend, Cartier Foster, made a wooden ukulele for him in Foster's shop class at school. Thrilled by the surprise but short of money to purchase accessories for his ukulele, Smith soaked cotton strings in water to render them turgid and used them as ukulele strings. Subsequently, he obtained a paper route and purchased proper ukulele strings.

His musical acumen was discovered a few years later. One day, his father unexpectedly returned home from work early and witnessed a crowd of people standing on his front lawn. Alarmed, he hurried to his house to investigate the commotion, and to his surprise, he saw young Smith playing the ukulele on his front porch as spectators threw nickels in his cap. Immediately, he took Smith to the Huntley music store at 517 Locust Street and purchased a Gibson banjo-ukulele for forty-five dollars.

During many nights during the late 1920s, Smith listened to a radio program that featured the Saunders Band and was broadcast from the Edgewater Hotel in Chicago. He also enjoyed the seventy-eight records from his brothers Herbert and Richard's music collection. His favorite song was "Can't You Wait 'Till the Cows Come Home?" Later, Smith joined a group of neighborhood musicians, and his father named them the Rhythm Aces; they consisted of R. Delbert Galloway on mandolin, Charles Jenkins on the six-string guitar and Ed Shelton on bass. As their popularity increased, the group auditioned for the WIL radio station and won a fifteen-minute night spot following popular radio program *Dream Boat*, hosted by Frankllyn McCormick, who recorded the popular song "The Melody of Love" with the Wayne King Orchestra. The song was written by Hanns Engelmann in 1903. On one occasion, the group played a private party at the Nugent House for the Anheuser-Busch family, the millionaire beer brewers whose corporate office was located in St. Louis. Internationally known bandleader Paul Whiteman sat in the audience and watched Smith intently. At intermission, Whiteman approached him and declared, "Son, if you were a white boy, I would have to pay you $5,000 a week."

In 1936, Smith joined the Jeter-Pillars Club Plantation band, led by alto saxophonist James Jeter and tenor saxophonist and front man Hayes Pillar. Once a week, they performed on a midnight excursion on the steamer *St. Paul* on the Mississippi River, restricted to black patrons. Many of the wealthy blacks of St. Louis and neighboring states frequented these cruises.

During the 1930s, Smith performed and traveled with a territorial band that performed one-night engagements in the Midwest and the South called

Eddie Johnson's Crackerjacks. Later, he was a member of the Sunset Royal Orchestra and played behind a touring African American modeling troupe called the Brown Skin Models. His big break came when he joined the immensely popular Andy Kirk and His Clouds of Joy, with which he recorded his signature song, "Floyd's Guitar Blues," in 1939. While serving in World War II, Kirk reserved Smith's seat in the string section of his orchestra, and Smith reclaimed the seat when he returned to civilian life.

In March 1965, Smith had an engagement at a jazz club in Buffalo, New York, where he met Dottie Clark, a native of Washington, D.C., and a former background singer of bandleader Ray Charles's all-female Raelettes. He auditioned and hired her and brought her to Indianapolis, where he obtained an engagement at the Hub Bub Night Club on Thirteenth Street. Smith signed an entertainment contract for two weeks and stayed there for four months. In 1965, he performed at the Hub Bub with Clark, organist Jackie Ivory and drummer Chino, and subsequently, Smith went to the Pink Poodle on Indianapolis's south side and performed with Jackie Ivory and drummer Harold Cardwell. Later in Indianapolis, he recorded with rhythm-and-blues performers organists Bill Doggett and Hank Marr. He was an original member of the Wild Bill Davis Trio. He joined the disco era by producing and then marrying disco diva Loleatta Holloway in the 1970s. Floyd Smith died on March 29, 1982, in Indianapolis.

Another proud Missourian who arrived on Indiana Avenue after being discharged from military service was Mingo Jones. Mingo Julian Jones was born on December 16, 1928, to Mingo Felix and Maudell Martin Jones in St. Joseph, Missouri. His father attended the Jenkins School of Music and was a professional trumpeter who played in clubs locally and in Kansas City, Missouri. His uncle Harry Martin, a tenor saxophonist, was a childhood schoolmate of internationally known saxophonist Coleman Hawkins and had his own orchestra. Hawkins played in Martin's band. Jones's earliest music instruction began while he was a student in the sixth grade at Lincoln Elementary School. His father taught him the basic rudiments of the trumpet and continued to tutor him until the outbreak of World War II, when his father sought employment at the local meatpacking plant. Martin continued to tutor him until he entered high school.

In 1942, Jones entered Bartlett High School and began his music education under the supervision of bandmaster Aurelius Whaley. "He was a dedicated teacher who demanded the best from each student," Jones recalled. Whaley engaged his band students in the Missouri black high school music competition.

Mingo Jones, a Missouri-born bassist who regularly performed with and was a favorite sideman of Wes Montgomery.

This annual event, which was sponsored by Lincoln University in Jefferson City, Missouri, invited bands from around the state to compete for prizes in music education. In 1946, Jones's band won third place in this competition.

The following year, Jones was employed as a waiter at the Rosecrans Army Air Force Base on the outskirts of St. Joseph. Generally, he waited tables and watched as bands entertained in the club. In 1945, his uncle Bruce James moved to Indiana and sought employment at the Ulen Country Club in Lebanon, and subsequently, he asked Jones to come to Indiana for the summer and seek employment. Jones agreed, and while in Indiana, he went to the Pearson Music School to explore the possibility of receiving music instruction. There he met Ray Churchman, a white drummer and bandleader who had once played with the Hampton Family Band. They developed a friendship, and both often went to the jazz performances at the Philharmonic Music Programs at the Murat Temple in downtown Indianapolis, where they saw stars such as bassist Ray Brown, pianist Oscar Peterson, tenor saxophonists Coleman Hawkins and Illinois Jacquet and trumpeter and composer Joe Newman.

In 1947, Jones enrolled in the Pearson School of Music with the intention to prepare to enter the Jordan College of Music. However, before he began his studies, he volunteered to join the United States Army in December 1948. In consideration of his music education background, he was advised to request that he be assigned to one of the several black military music schools around the country. He auditioned, passed the test with "flying colors" and went to the Fort Dix Army Base in New Jersey to join the 173rd Army Band. In 1949, while serving in Japan, he was given the option of selecting a secondary instrument, and he chose the bass. In June 1948, he became a member of General Douglas McArthur's 8th Army Brigade Band and performed near Yokohama, Japan.

After the war, in 1952, Jones returned to Indianapolis and ventured onto the Avenue to the surprise of everyone. Everyone knew him earlier when he frequented Indiana Avenue before he entered military service, but they did not know to where he had disappeared. His first gig on Indiana Avenue was playing bass with guitarist Wes Montgomery, pianist Erroll Grandy, tenor saxophonist "Pookie" Johnson and drummer Sonny Johnson, as well as bandleader Dudley Storms, at the Fort Benjamin Harrison Officer's Club. Later, he performed with bassist Leroy Vinnegar and pianist Buddy Montgomery in the Dudley Storms Band and then went to the Ferguson Hotel and performed with pianist Carl Perkins and bassist Phillip "Flip" Stewart. His first big touring date came when he hit the road with Jimmy Coe's Orchestra and played around Philadelphia and New York from 1953 until 1957. Returning to Indianapolis, Jones performed with other musicians, such as trumpeter Lewis Hughes, drummers Carroll Engs and Count Fisher and tenor saxophonist "Pookie" Johnson. Jones was inducted into the Indianapolis Jazz Foundation's Hall of Fame on December 3, 2001. He received the Ralph Adams Life Time Achievement Award in 2009 and the Juneteenth Jazz Legacy Award in 2011.

Some music students had the language of jazz in their blood, seemingly a component of their DNA. John Boyd Shacklett was born on June 20, 1937, to Boyd Thomas Shacklett and Clara Virginia Watts in Indianapolis. His mother was an educator who played the piano and hailed from a family of entertainers that included her brother, Billy Watts, who was a dancer with the original Manhattan Duo, a song-and-dance team that included Charles Burton. The team performed on New York's Great White Way during the vaudeville era, and Watts was a major influence on legendary dancer Bill "Bojangles" Robinson.

Early in her life, Shacklett's mother desired to pursue a career in the entertainment industry; however, being a member of a matriarchal family of educators, she was discouraged and was determined to make that opportunity available to her son. To develop his artistic talents, she purchased his first guitar shortly after he graduated from grade school.

In the early 1950s, Shacklett attended Crispus Attucks High School and found himself not particularly interested in the rigors of obtaining a high school education. Expressing his thoughts about school, he once said, "I really wasn't motivated to study the standard high school curriculum being that my mother and her family were all educators. I had gone through that curriculum long before entering high school." During his freshman year, he left school and traveled to another institution of higher learning, the Indianapolis Public Library. There, he read every book available on guitar instruction and advanced harmony. He sought local guitar training and was introduced to John Watson, who was purported to be one of the original Ink Spots. Next, Shacklett received technical guitar instruction from pianist Erroll Grandy, who mentored many of the blossoming musicians on Indiana Avenue, including guitarist Wes Montgomery.

One day, while walking down the Avenue, Shacklett crossed the bridge over the canal on Indiana Avenue and heard the most mystifying version of the old standard "Dark Eyes" that he had ever heard. Initially, he thought that it was someone's radio blaring from a window on a hot summer day, but as he followed the sound, he saw a hazy image of a man with a guitar strapped across his shoulder. That man was Edward Lamonte "Guitar Pete" Franklin, considered one of the most unique and innovative blues guitarists. He mentored Shacklett and exposed him to every blues progression and old jazz standard in a few months. Franklin's instruction ignited a burning desire in Shacklett to continue his quest to master the guitar.

Franklin then introduced Shacklett to guitarist Carl Moore, who taught Shacklett the rudiments and aesthetics required for mastering advanced chords and recommended instructional material by music theorist Mickey Baker. Moore also encouraged Shacklett to study the Schillinger system of music as a source for stimulating creative ideas that helped him in formulating advanced harmonic material. Shacklett was also inspired and tutored by guitarist Johnny Blanchard, who impressed on him the value of driving melodic solos with substantive content. "He was sharing and helpful and helped me along during a time when a lot of folks didn't share," Shacklett related.

After studying the technical aspects of playing the guitar, Shacklett was eager to apply his theoretical knowledge to an actual performance on the bandstand. He decided to test his chops on Indiana Avenue and discovered guitarist Wes Montgomery. Montgomery became a mentor and, on many occasions, invited Shacklett to sit in with him at Jacque Durham's Missile Room, George's Bar and the Hub Bub. There, Shacklett played with other musicians such as trumpeters Freddie Hubbard, Virgil Jones and Maceo Hampton; saxophonist James Spaulding; pianists Melvin Rhyne, Earl Van Riper and Erman Hubbard; bassists Mingo Jones and Larry Ridley; drummer Paul Parker; and vibraphonist/baritone saxophonist Duke Hampton.

In 1954, Shacklett left Indianapolis to tour with bandleader Hiawatha Edmondson, who wrote many of the arrangements for the Count Basie Orchestra. This national tour led him to the East Coast, where he reunited with many of his aforementioned Indianapolis band mates and many internationally known stars. Shacklett shared the stage with musicians such as tenor/alto saxophonists Rahsaan Roland Kirk and Eddie "Clean Head" Vinson, vocalists Nancy Wilson and Arthur Prysock, pianist/organist Don Patterson, drummer "Killer Ray" Appleton and vibraphonist Lem Winchester.

In 1960, Shacklett's professional career was abruptly interrupted when he was drafted into the United States Army; however, this drastic change in his life did not affect the momentum of his musical career. He maintained his fascination with the guitar by competing in four worldwide air force talent contests in which he won four "Oscars" as a solo virtuoso guitarist.

After Shacklett's discharge from the service in 1968, Wes Montgomery died, and Shacklett took over the Wes Montgomery Trio, which included organist/pianist Melvin Rhyne and drummers "Killer Ray" Appleton and occasionally Ronnie Rhyne. Shacklett then redirected his music career toward teaching, and in conjunction with the University of Wisconsin–Madison, he privately taught graduate students advanced theoretical jazz and the disciplines of jazz theory and professional performance at Malcolm Shabazz High School.

In 1975, Shacklett accepted a professorship at Norfolk State University of Virginia and initiated a Music in the Media program that included all aspects of jazz education. He taught and mentored many students who would later distinguish themselves in the world of music. Shacklett continues to perform and teach in his music academy in the state of Washington.

One of Johnny Shacklett's most prominent music instructors and mentors to whom he always expressed his most sincere gratitude was John Blanchard. Blanchard was born in Detroit, Michigan, the son of a Frenchman from Quebec, Canada, and an African American woman. His father placed his children in a home for orphans and deserted him when Blanchard was a small child.

In the 1920s, Blanchard moved to Indianapolis to live with his aunt, Kate Price, on Patterson Street near Indiana Avenue and attended William D. McCoy Elementary School 24. He was not motivated to excel in school but developed a love for jazz and popular music that attracted him

Johnny Blanchard, a jazz guitarist who mentored Wes Montgomery and taught him basic chords. He was known for his kind and gentle spirit in sharing his knowledge with younger guitarists. *Courtesy of Larry Goshen.*

to Indiana Avenue. As a young man, he met Jerry Daniels and Simp Green, two individuals who were instrumental in his early music career. Daniels was an original member of the world-famous Ink Spots vocal quintet, and Simp Green was a guitarist and tap dancer employed by the William H. Block Department Store as an advertiser and shopping window model. According to Blanchard, "He was outfitted in the most fashionable attire of the day and tap-danced in the shopping room window as pedestrians passed by." Green taught Blanchard the basic chords on the guitar and introduced him to many of the nightclub owners on the Avenue. Daniels was his guitar instructor at the McArthur's Conservatory of Music.

During World War II, Blanchard served in the United States Army and was assigned to Special Service duty as an entertainer. There he met his cousin Thad Jones, trumpeter, conductor and composer from Pontiac, Michigan, and traveled all around the country entertaining troops at various military installations. After the war, he returned to Indianapolis and got a gig at the P&P Club on Indiana Avenue, where he performed nightly. Blanchard humorously recalled that one night while performing, a young man entered the club carrying an ES-125 guitar with one of the keys missing and a pair of pliers that he used to tighten the strings. He placed his guitar on the stairs and listened attentively as Blanchard completed the first set. During intermission, the young man approached Blanchard, introduced himself and confessed, "I've been listening to you play those double octaves and I can't figure out how you do it. Can you teach me how?" Blanchard agreed and later taught a young Wes Montgomery the chords, and he was also responsible for getting Wes an engagement date at the club.

During Blanchard's heyday on Indiana Avenue, he performed with organist "Brother" Jack McDuff at George's Bar and later traveled off the Avenue to the Brass Rail Nightclub downtown on Ohio Street, backing risqué blues singer Ophelia Hoy. In New York, he performed with country guitarist/banjoist Roy Clark at Carnegie Hall. John Blanchard died on September 28, 2010.

As Blanchard traveled up and down Indiana Avenue, performing in many of its hottest jazz clubs, he encountered and befriended two budding jazz guitarists who established themselves among the Avenue's finest musicians: Paul Weeden and Alec Stephens. Weeden was born on January 7, 1928, to John Thomas Weeden Sr. and Gladys Mae Evans Weeden in Indianapolis. His father was a minister at the First Baptist Church of West Indianapolis, and he was raised in a very religious environment. He attended Crispus Attucks High School and was mentored by Russell Brown and Norman Merrifield. As a guitarist, he performed with musicians such as trombonist David Baker, tenor saxophonist Jimmy Coe, bassist Leroy Vinnegar and drummers Al Coleman and Mingo Jones in many of the jazz venues on Indiana Avenue.

In 1966, he relocated to Stockholm, Sweden, where he accepted a teaching position at a music academy. Later, he moved to Oslo, Norway, and continued his teaching career, eventually launching a professional recording career. He performed in many of Oslo's jazz festivals and made several films in which he spoke Norwegian. Paul Weeden died on July 2, 2011, in Oslo.

Another fellow jazz guitarist who cut his teeth with Blanchard and Weeden on Indiana Avenue was Alec Stephens. In the early 1950s, many Indiana Avenue patrons acknowledged the genius of the guitar giant Charlie Christian, and Stephens was greatly influenced by Christian as well. Cecil Alec Stephens was born in Indianapolis on January 24, 1922. He was the

Paul Weeden, a jazz guitarist who began performing on the Avenue during the Wes Montgomery era but went to Sweden to record. He performed and taught in Norway. He also filmed movies in which he spoke Norwegian.

fifth of seven children born to Cato and Lillie Belle Malone Stephens. He developed a love for music as a small child after listening to his father, an accomplished musician, play a mandolin around the house. He first practiced with the mandolin, and after polishing his technique, he did odd jobs around the neighborhood to save money to purchase a guitar. After graduating to the guitar, he joined other musically inclined friends from the neighborhood and played in many of the clubs on Indiana Avenue. As he gained a reputation for excellence on the guitar, he tutored some up-and-coming guitar players who later made indelible marks in the world of music. One of the people was a young lad by the name of Wes Montgomery.

Stephens relocated to Miami, Florida, and worked for several years as a leader of the house band for the Rockland Palace Night Club. Alec Stephens died on December 27, 1988, in Indianapolis.

Chapter 10

Here Come the Young Turks

The early 1950s was a time of heightened excitement and great anticipation among jazz aficionados on Indiana Avenue. The bebop era of jazz, which began in the early 1940s, had introduced a more complex, syncopated, medium- to faster-tempo music characterized by instrumental virtuosity and experimental improvisation. This musical approach to improvisation hit the jazz scene like a ton of bricks. Artists like trumpeters Dizzy Gillespie and Miles Davis, alto/tenor saxophonist Charlie Parker, pianists Bud Powell and Thelonious Monk and drummers Max Roach and Kenny Clarke were among the major innovators of this new musical genre, and their influence on the music scene was universally acclaimed. Many of the Indianapolis high school music students traveled to the Avenue and stood outside the Sunset Terrace Ballroom, the Cotton Club and Henri's just to get a glimpse of and hear the music of these jazz giants. So inspired were these "young Turks" that they organized jazz aggregations and jam sessions to explore this new music genre. One group of youngsters that included Freddie Hubbard on trumpet, Earmon Hubbard on piano, James Spaulding on alto saxophone, Virgil Jones on trumpet, Paul Parker on drums and Larry Ridley on bass practiced for hours until they captured the true essence of the music. Bebop had arrived, and everybody was digging it.

Freddie Hubbard became the most notable of the young jazz performers who traveled to Indiana Avenue and sneaked into the nightclubs to watch veteran jazz entertainers perform, later climbing to the top of the jazz world as a stylist who set new standards on the trumpet. Frederick Dewayne Hubbard was born

Freddie Hubbard, considered by jazz historians one of the two greatest trumpeters in jazz history along with Miles Davis. Hubbard won a Grammy Award.

on April 7, 1938, in Indianapolis to Earmon Hubbard Sr. and Delphia Hubbard. He received some of his early music training under the tutelage of John H. White, a music instructor at Arsenal Technical High School. Early in Hubbard's musical training, White did not permit him to play the trumpet. Because White did not approve of Hubbard's technique of fingering the keys, he insisted that Hubbard begin his musical training on the flugelhorn. Eventually, after Hubbard improved his technique to the satisfaction of White, he was permitted to play a trumpet that was given to him by a schoolmate, Albert Moore. Hubbard quickly became the premier instrumentalist in his class. At the funeral of John White, Hubbard eulogized him by stating, "Had it not been for his insistence that I play the flugelhorn, and then I would not have reached the ultimate level of greatness."

John White was instrumental in Hubbard's receiving a music scholarship to study French horn at Indiana Central College (now the University of Indianapolis); however, Hubbard opted to concentrate on the trumpet at Butler University. The music curriculum at Butler University emphasized classical music, and this irritated Hubbard since he desired to explore the world of jazz. It's not surprising that his tenure there was short-lived. To satisfy his appetite for jazz, Hubbard joined his band mate Larry Ridley and studied music at the Arthur Jordan Conservatory of Music. After class, on many occasions, Hubbard, Ridley and trombonist Dave Baker would sneak into the music rehearsal room and experiment with the most recent sounds in jazz. On several occasions, they were warned to refrain from playing this kind of music, but they did not acquiesce. Finally, they were expelled from the institution. Later, Hubbard studied with Max Woodbury, who occupied the trumpet chair with the Indianapolis Symphony Orchestra.

Hubbard relocated to New York in 1958 and immediately obtained a spot in saxophonist John Coltrane's group while rooming with trumpeter Eric

Dolphy. He later teamed with drummer "Philly" Joe Jones. While Hubbard was performing at Bird Land, a critically observant trumpeter named Miles Davis was sitting in the audience. Despite the pressure of performing before an iconic figure, Hubbard relaxed, took control of the moment and presented a spectacular performance. So impressed was Davis that he immediately left his seat, ran to the nearest telephone, called Alfred Lion of Blue Note Records and informed him of the potential of "this young dude from 'Naptown.'" Hubbard signed with Alfred Lion and remained on that label until 1965.

During the 1960s, Hubbard's star ascended as he performed with some of the greatest jazz groups of the period. He joined Art Blakey's Jazz Messengers and occupied the chair of departing trumpeter Lee Morgan. In the mid-1960s, Hubbard worked steadily with drummer Max Roach and tenor saxophonist Sonny Rollins. With the momentum generated by his association with such icons of jazz, Hubbard's star continued to rise, and by the early 1970s, he was among the top jazz trumpeters in the world. His 1972 album *First Light* won a Grammy for best jazz performance of the year.

In the late 1980s, Hubbard's star began to descend as he was beset by a number of problems. First, he developed a cancerous growth on his lip that impeded his ability to hit those special high notes, and this caused Hubbard a great deal of emotional distress. After having the growth surgically removed, he was never able to recapture his glory days and hit those soaring notes that were so characteristic of his earlier works of art. He also suffered the emotional effects of substance abuse and personal problems and developed a troublesome reputation in regards to making performance engagements. Hubbard died on December 29, 2008, in Sherman Oaks, California.

Although Hubbard lived on the east side of Indianapolis and had to travel a few miles to jam with his jazz cohorts on Indiana Avenue, others lived in proximity to one another. In the late 1940s and early 1950s, there were several young jazz students who lived in the Lockefield Gardens Housing Development near Indiana Avenue. They were influenced by the culture of jazz that permeated the atmosphere and the sounds of jazz that emanated from many of the nightclubs and record shops along the entertainment corridor. Some followed their dreams by focusing their attention and instruction on the jazz artists who performed in the clubs and adhered closely to the rudiments of the traditional jazz genre. Others took a different direction and incorporated classical music education in their course of study in the hopes of realizing their dreams to become jazz performers. One such jazz performer was Larry Ridley.

Laurence "Larry" Howard Ridley II was born on September 3, 1937, to Laurence and Nevoleane Morris Ridley in Indianapolis. His family loved jazz and other genres of music, all of which he heard constantly in his home. Young Ridley was first inspired to learn the violin through hearing Jascha Heifetz on the *Bell Telephone Hour* radio program in 1942. The news of his desire to study and play music spread throughout the family. Fortunately, he had a relative who was employed by Pearson's Music Store, and this enabled Ridley's mother to purchase his first musical instrument, a small violin, for ten dollars. He began taking music lessons from Ruth McArthur, who charged his mother seventy-five cents per lesson.

Miss McArthur was inspired to create a music school by her training as a student under J. Harold Brown, head of the music department at Crispus Attucks High School. She was responsible for introducing music training to African American students in Indianapolis's segregated public school system. The Ruth McArthur Conservatory of Music was supported by her contacts with the Indianapolis Symphony Orchestra and the first violinist with the orchestra, Mildred Lind, who became Ridley's second teacher after Miss McArthur.

Ridley's parents instilled a work ethic in him and his brother. At the age of six, he and his younger brother, Michael, were altar boys at Bethel African Methodist Episcopal Church, and they assisted their father in delivering the *Indianapolis Star* newspaper on an early morning route. They also delivered coal and ice, moved furniture and did other odd jobs with their father in his 1937 Chevrolet pickup truck. Ridley also found opportunities to dazzle the appreciative music public with his early skills, including at the pulpit at Bethel AME Church. One of his earliest public performances as a youngster was held during church service when he performed "Ave Maria" on violin accompanied by Olivia McGee on piano. The early twentieth-century musician and songwriter Ben Holliman, who was the father of his Uncle Thomas Ridley's wife, Louise, tutored him on the finer aspects of early jazz and boogie-woogie blues music. Holliman was also a melody collaborator with Hoagy Carmichael on the song "Stardust," for which, according to Ridley, he never officially received writer's credit. Carmichael would occasionally stop by and lay a few dollars on him. "Uncle Ben" used an early paper disc recorder to record an impromptu jam session with Larry on violin and Holliman on the guitar playing boogie-woogie blues.

Although Ridley did not attend Crispus Attucks High School, he was encouraged by its music instructors Russell Brown, Norman Merrifield and LaVerne Newsome. Many of these instructors were closely associated with the McArthur Conservatory of Music and would periodically lend assistance in music instruction. Ridley organized a jazz band in 1957 that he christened the Jazz Contemporaries, composed of some of the outstanding young musicians in the city. The group included Freddie Hubbard on trumpet; James Spaulding on flute, alto and tenor saxophones; Paul Parker on drums; and Walter Miller (and later Al Plank) on piano. Although he and most of the players were underage, they performed at George's Bar, one of the hottest jazz spots on Indiana Avenue. Ridley's

Larry Ridley, a bassist who created the jazz department at Rutgers University. *Courtesy of Larry Ridley.*

uncles Martin and Thomas Ridley knew the owner, Leo Lesser, and secured the job for the group. The group played six nights a week with two matinees during the summer months in 1957. A fan in the audience recorded one of their performances on a Webcor Wire Recorder during that period, and fifty years later, the recording was unearthed by a graduate music student at Indiana University and presented to jazz professor David Baker.

Always wanting to learn more and continue to develop his craft, Ridley met Fender bassist Monk Montgomery on the street one day and requested music lessons. Montgomery agreed and asked Ridley to come to his house later in the week. When Ridley arrived, he was shocked to discover Wes Montgomery on guitar, Buddy Montgomery on piano, Sonny Johnson on drums and Pookie Johnson on tenor saxophone. Monk informed Ridley that he would be traveling to California to complete some business matters in forming a jazz group called the Mastersounds. He asked Ridley to temporarily replace him on bass so that the Montgomery-Johnson Quintet could continue to perform at the Turf Club on West Sixteenth Street. After playing some of the tunes with the musicians, who made him feel comfortable, Ridley agreed.

Ridley's first road gig was at age sixteen, playing with trumpeter Conte Candoli, who put together a quartet with Slide Hampton on piano and trombone, Benny Barth on drums and Ridley on bass. They played nightly for a few months at the Club Shaeferee in South Bend.

In 1955, after graduation from high school, with the help of music educator Dr. Roscoe Polin, Ridley obtained a violin scholarship at the Indiana University School of Music in Bloomington, Indiana. While attending the university, Ridley formed a jazz quartet composed of Joe Hunt on drums, Paul Plummer on tenor saxophone and Austin Crowe on piano. They traveled to Indianapolis and performed at the immensely popular Clown's Playhouse on the city's south side. Gunther Schuller of the Metropolitan Opera Orchestra of New York, while visiting Indiana University in 1959, witnessed Ridley's performance with the David Baker Band. Schuller offered Ridley, Baker and Alan Kiger scholarships to further their jazz studies at the Lenox School of Jazz in Lenox, Massachusetts. There they studied with pianist, composer and theorist George Russell; jazz critic and musicologist Marshall Stearns; trumpeter Kenny Dorham; composer and arranger Bill Russo; drummer Max Roach; pianist Bill Evans; and others. Ridley rehearsed, played and performed in a group that included alto saxophonist Ornette Coleman and cornetist Don Cherry. Ridley relocated to New York City in 1960 and joined the Slide Hampton Octet.

During a professional career that has spanned more than five decades, Ridley has performed, toured and recorded with a who's who of American jazz history. Legendary stars such as pianist/composer Duke Ellington, pianist Thelonious Monk, trumpeter Dizzy Gillespie, tenor saxophonist Benny Gholson, trumpeter Art Farmer and many others have called on him to infuse creativity and ensure the artistic integrity of their projects. From 1971 until 1999, he was professor of music at Rutgers, the State University of New Jersey. He also served as chairman of the music department at Rutgers/Livingston College and chief architect of the jazz performance degree programs at both institutions. Ridley completed his undergraduate degree at New York University, his master's degree at the State University of New York/Empire State College and his honorary Doctor of Performing Arts at the University of Maryland Eastern Shore in 2005. In 1998, he was inducted into the International Association of Jazz Educators Hall of Fame and the *Down Beat* magazine Jazz Educators Hall of Fame. Two years later, he was the recipient of the Benny Gholson Award at Howard University. Ridley served as the executive director of the African American Jazz Caucus and Jazz Artist in Residence at the Schomburg Center in Harlem, New York.

Larry Ridley's musical odyssey down Indiana Avenue inspired his younger brother to follow suit. Michael Elliot Ridley was born on April 4, 1939, in Indianapolis, the second of four children who were raised in an environment in which there was a premium placed on excellence in music performance. He received his early music education at William D. McCoy School 24, located in the Lockefield Gardens Housing Development, and the MacArthur Conservatory of Music on Indiana Avenue. He studied the trumpet and was a member of the band at Shortridge High School, from which he graduated in 1956.

After high school, Michael Ridley journeyed to Indiana Avenue and performed with the Dudley Storms Orchestra in many of the jazz hot spots. He served in the military in 1959 and was selected to join the United States

Michael Ridley, a dynamic and renowned trumpeter who left the Avenue and dazzled New York jazz aficionados in the nightclubs and classrooms. *Courtesy of Dorothy Ridley.*

Army 266th Band at Fort Hood, Texas. After his discharge from military service, he followed his dream to become a musician in New York. Beginning his professional career, he recorded and toured with soul music stars James Brown, Otis Redding and Wilson Pickett, as well as Motown vocal greats Diana Ross, Stevie Wonder and Mary Wells. He was an experienced jazz musician who worked with the Hank Johnson Quartet, the Dave Carter Ensemble, saxophonists Frank Foster and Archie Shepp and organist Jimmy McGriff. He was a professor of music at Rutgers/Livingston College. Michael Ridley died on May 8, 2011.

One of the Ridley brothers' schoolyard playmates who lived less than a few hundred yards from Ridley's residence in the Lockefield Gardens Housing Development was James Spaulding. Both attended William D. McCoy School 24, where they were introduced to the world of music. There's an old saying that the apple doesn't fall too far from the tree, and James Ralph Spaulding Jr. was one jazz student who followed in his father's footsteps. Born to James Ralph Sr. and Mae Paul Flournoy Spaulding on July 30, 1937, in Indianapolis, he was constantly exposed to jazz and swing music. His father was a professional jazz guitarist who traveled throughout the state with a group called the Brown Buddies, former Crispus Attucks music students who named themselves in tribute to their beloved mentor and music instructor, Harold Brown. His father brought home the most outstanding records of the day that featured entertainment notables such as tenor saxophonists Charlie Parker and Lester Young and vocalists Billie Holiday, Nat King Cole and Billy Eckstein, and he would discuss the various elements of their musical style with his wide-eyed, inquisitive son. While a grade school student at William D. McCoy School 24, Spaulding Jr. was instructed by music teacher Miss Anna White.

Upon entering Crispus Attucks High School, he enrolled in music courses and met band director Russell Brown. Brown saw so much promise in young Spaulding's music ability that he convinced him to join the band. He later became the drum major of the marching band. Then Spaulding realized a tugging in his soul that was probably prompted by his musical instruction from his father. He wanted desperately to play the saxophone. Fortunately, one of his classmates had purchased a used saxophone but, after a few weeks of practice, had tired of the instrument and trotted off to the football field. Spaulding was made aware of the situation and purchased the saxophone for ten dollars. He fondly remembered the time and commitment that Russell Brown invested in each music student at Crispus Attucks: "Russell Brown very graciously and unselfishly gave of his time to all of his students that were so inclined to remain after school to play this music." Some of those students included Albert

James Spaulding, a saxophonist who performed on Indiana Avenue with Sun Ra.

Walton on piano and Virgil Jones and David Hardiman on trumpet. His friend Albert Walton taught Spaulding the saxophone fingering techniques. Spaulding entered military service in 1955 and was stationed at Fort Benjamin Harrison in Indianapolis.

While in the army, Spaulding was recruited by Larry Ridley to join the Jazz Contemporaries. Ridley desperately needed Spaulding to occupy the saxophone chair to ensure the creativity of the group, so he devised an ingenious plan that saved the day. Ridley advertised the group's engagements in the *Indianapolis Recorder* newspaper, listed all of the musicians by name and then added a special guest, "Brother Spee Abdul Malik." This was the pseudonym for Spaulding, employed so that the military would not be aware of his nocturnal moonlighting. They performed to standing room–only engagements at George's Bar.

After his discharge from the army in 1957, Spaulding relocated to Chicago and began taking courses in music theory at the Cosmopolitan School of Music at night. While a student, he discovered that one of the workers in the building was the mother of one of his jazz idols, the legendary saxophonist Johnny Griffin. He excitedly requested her to introduce him to her famous son, and she did so. One evening, Spaulding drove to the wildly popular Flame Bar on Chicago's south side. There, on stage, he saw his idol Johnny Griffin "blowing and fingering some of the fastest and most melodic notes imaginable," according to Spaulding. At intermission, he approached Griffin and bombarded him with seemingly a million questions relative to jazz theory and other esoteric topics. Griffin responded, "Man, just play what you feel deep inside of your soul and be done with it." By a stroke of luck, Spaulding was breakfast jamming at Chicago's Pershing Hotel when in strolled bandleader, composer and pianist Sun Ra. After the first set, Sun Ra approached James and asked him to come to an audition. Spaulding went and was hired on the spot. He made his first recording in Chicago circa 1957 on the Chess label with Jerry Butler singing "Lost."

In 1962, Spaulding arrived in New York City and made his first recording as a sideman on a Freddie Hubbard album entitled *Hub Tones* on the Blue Note label. He also played with pianist Randy Weston and drummer Max Roach. In the late 1960s, James attended Livingston College and Rutgers University, where he taught flute as an adjunct professor. While attending Livingston College, he became a member of the Duke Ellington Orchestra but left to complete his education. His original music, a suite entitled "A Song of Courage," was performed by him with a complete orchestra and choir at the Voorhees Chapel at Rutgers University. This concert was funded by the National Endowment for the Arts. In 1975, he received his Bachelor of Music Education degree.

Spaulding has been a member of the Freddie Hubbard Quintet, the Sun Ra Arkestra, the Duke Ellington Big Band, the David Murray Octet and Big Band and the World Saxophone Quartet.

On July 30, 2001, he performed at the Saxophone Summit Harlem Celebration marking the opening of former president Bill Clinton's new office on 125th Street. On February 22, 2002, he was one of the judges at the Thelonious Monk International Jazz Competition. Spaulding has been playing professionally since age ten. During his long career, the range of his performance experience has extended nationally and internationally. He appeared at the Montpelier and Saalfelden Jazz Festivals and has been recorded on more than one hundred albums with legendary musicians ranging from Sun Ra to Louis Armstrong. He has appeared on the Blue Note label with artists such as tenor saxophonists Wayne Shorter, Hank Mobley, Stanley Turrentine and Sam Rivers and pianists Horace Silver, McCoy Tyner and Duke Pearson. In 2000, James recorded three live albums with his band at the Up and Over Jazz Café, Brooklyn, New York, under his own label: *Speetone Music Volume One*, *Blues Up and Over Volume Two* and *Round to It.*

Another young jazz student who lived in the Lockefield Gardens Housing Development along with Larry Ridley and James Spaulding was trumpeter Virgil Jones. Virgil Jones Jr. was born on August 26, 1939, to Virgil Sr. and Lucille Lucas Jones in Indianapolis. He was constantly exposed to the various kinds of music that accentuated the atmosphere along that long stretch of entertainment establishments. Like Spaulding, Jones attended School 24 and then Booker T. Washington School 17, where his first music teacher was Russell Brown. Brown was always amazed at Jones's perfect pitch on his trumpet but still insisted that he read music as well. Concerning Brown, Jones related, "He must have been a good teacher because I never had a private lesson and I sight read very well."

In 1952, Jones entered Crispus Attucks High School and joined the band and orchestra under Brown. He became an outstanding honor roll student who scored in the upper 10 percent on the National Scholastic Achievement Examination. At the age of fifteen, Jones refused a four-year science scholarship to Morehouse College, preferring to graduate from Crispus Attucks. During his senior year, trombonist David Baker was a student teacher at Attucks, and this relationship became very significant in Jones's jazz career.

During Jones's formative years as a musician, he would often go to Jacque Durham's Missile Room, located near Indiana Avenue. There, he listened attentively to the up-and-coming jazz guitarist Wes Montgomery.

Jones related that the most enjoyable aspect of his early music education was jamming at George's Bar and other Indiana Avenue nightspots. Referring to his musical experience, he said, "Many of us would travel in groups to Chicago to hear such popular jazz musicians as trumpeters Miles Davis and Kenny Dorham, tenor saxophonists John Coltrane and Hank Mobley, drummers Max Roach and Philly Joe Jones and bassists Paul Chambers and George Morrow."

After high school graduation, his first gig was playing in the David Baker Big Band at the French Lick Jazz Festival in 1958. Two years later, Baker recommended him to Lionel

Virgil Jones, a trumpeter who was one of Russell Brown's favorite students. He read music like a professional while in high school, according to Brown. He was a member of Dick Cavett's television orchestra. *Courtesy of Nathan and Marcia Jones-Wimberly.*

Hampton, and Jones joined his band. In 1960, Jones traveled with the Hampton band to New York City and later toured the United States, Europe, Argentina and Japan. Some of Jones's earliest recordings were with Milt Jackson's *Invitation Album* in 1962, Roland Kirk's *Reeds and Deeds* in 1963, *Slightly Latin* in 1966 and Charles Earland's *Black Talk* in 1969.

Jones expanded his entertainment horizon by exploring different outlets, such as Broadway productions, television and the cabaret music circuit. In 1973, he played in the house band that backed Hollywood actress Debbie Reynolds in her Broadway debut of *Irene*. He also provided music for such Broadway hits as *Ain't Misbehavin'*, *Jelly's Last Jam* and *Big Time Buck White* (which starred world heavyweight boxing champion Muhammad Ali), as well as *Black and Blue*, which highlighted the return of rhythm-and-blues diva Ruth Brown to the bright lights of Broadway. For seven years, he performed with cabaret singer and pianist Bobby Short at the Carlyle Hotel. He was also a member of the house band for the Dick Cavett television show for the

American Broadcasting Company. Later, he performed at the White House during the Clinton administration. In the 1990s, he performed with the Smithsonian Jazz Works Orchestra under the baton of David Baker. Jones died on April 20, 2012, in New York.

Al Finnell, a contemporary of Virgil Jones, was born on the east side of Indianapolis on December 31, 1935, to Alfred Finnell Sr. and Idovie Boyd Finnell. Young Finnell's family moved to the Lockefield Gardens Housing Development in 1939 when he was four years old. Like many youngsters, Finnell delighted himself in playing basketball, marbles and softball and riding his bicycle. He vividly remembered playing basketball with future Crispus Attucks basketball great Bailey Robertson,

Al Finnell flew under the entertainment radar for many years, but he proved to be an excellent Fender bassist very worthy of mention. *Courtesy of Mark Sheldon.*

who for years held many of the basketball records at Indiana Central College (University of Indianapolis), and brother Oscar Robertson, perennial all-star of the Cincinnati Royals and Milwaukee Bucks professional basketball teams and member of the National Basketball Association's Hall of Fame. On many hot summer days, he locked horns on the basketball dust bowl with Hallie Bryant, the high school Mr. Basketball of Indiana in 1953 and star basketball player at Indiana University and later with the Harlem Globetrotters.

Although Finnell passionately loved basketball and other childhood games popular with his playmates, he was also influenced by the music he was exposed to every day while doing his household chores. His father sang in the men's ensemble and church choir at Mount Zion and Mount Paran Baptist Churches, and his mother played the piano at home. She loved to play the piano and hum in unison with the radio; her favorite singers were Nat King Cole and Harry Belafonte.

Young Finnell attended William D. McCoy School 24, located in the housing development. His first elementary school music instructor was teacher and choir director Nellie Rogers, who recognized his music aptitude and encouraged him to sing in the choir. Loretta Miller Radcliffe, another music teacher, composed songs for young Finnell and his classmates and played records so that her class could sing along.

In 1947, Finnell entered the Mary E. Cable Elementary School located on Blackford Street only a few blocks east of Indiana Avenue. There he met recent college graduate and music educator Larry Liggett. Liggett taught instrumental music and introduced Finnell to playing the drums. Before Finnell was able to develop an appreciation for the drums, his family moved to the east side of town, where he attended John Hope School 26. There he met vocal music teacher Clara Kirk, who recognized his music ability and immediately placed him in the choir. On one occasion, Kirk took the choir to a music festival at Garfield Park, where his school competed with other choirs in the Indianapolis Public School system. The choir distinguished itself among the other choirs; after having sung a few numbers and receiving thunderous applause, several of the spectators approached Miss Kirk on the bandstand in total disbelief. They had never heard a thirteen-year-old youngster like Finnell sing bass!

In 1949, when Finnell entered Crispus Attucks High School, news of his musical ability had preceded him. Kirk had told choir director Norman Merrifield about Finnell because Merrifield was desperately searching for bass and baritone voices for the school choir. Merrifield immediately assigned Finnell to the a cappella choir, the boys' Glee Club and the Boys' Octet. Singing with the Boys' Octet, Finnell joined fellow classmates Chester Brown, Robert Wesley and James Lee, who formed the rhythm-and-blues quintet the Counts a few years later. Merrifield was so astonished by Finnell's musical aptitude that he tested him several times. Still, Finnell registered the highest score in the history of the school. Merrifield then referred Finnell to LaVerne Newsome, who taught string instruments. Finnell recalled, "He pointed to a brand-new bass sitting in the corner of his office and asked me if I wanted to play strings and said that I could keep it at home." Taking an instrument home was a rare occurrence at Crispus Attucks High School. Newsome recognized Finnell's innate ability and tutored him. In 1952, Newsome also recommended that he participate in the All-City Orchestra, composed of the school system's best music students. Finnell auditioned and was selected as one of the few African Americans in the string section—he was by far the most gifted string bass player, but he did not receive the first chair position.

In late August 1952, Finnell entered Indiana Central College and was immediately recruited to play in the string ensemble by Allan T. Schirmer.

Norman Merrifield, one of the three Crispus Attucks music professors who was responsible for development of many of the Indiana Avenue musicians. *Courtesy of Crispus Attucks Museum.*

That same year, he met fellow student saxophonist Al Officer, and they began to experiment with playing jazz. He and Officer joined young jazz aspirants Freddie Hubbard and his older brother Earmon at their home and practiced for many hours to sharpen their chops. Finnell accompanied Freddie Hubbard on a professional engagement at the Walker Casino in 1957.

In 1958, Finnell's father introduced him to his cousin James DuPee, tenor saxophone/organist and the father of saxophonist Alonzo "Pookie" Johnson. DuPee liked what he heard in rehearsal and invited Finnell to perform with him and his son, drummer Bobby Dupee, at the George Washington Carver Center in Kokomo. Later, Finnell performed with groups such as the Al Walton Quartet, which included Finnell on bass, Walton on tenor saxophone, Roland Armour on piano/organ and Eddie Johnson on drums. Finnell played with the Larry Liggett Orchestra for more than fifteen years and appeared at upscale Indianapolis supper clubs such as the Marrott Hotel, Stouffer's Inn and numerous country clubs.

When Finnell retired from an administrative position with the Indianapolis Public School system in 2000, he organized two groups, first the Mastertones and then the Indy Jazzmen. Both groups were composed of Finnell on bass guitar, Bill Penick on tenor saxophone, Joe Boyce on vibes, his son Vincent Finnell on drums, Craig Hicks on keyboards and Barbara Randall on vocals.

Chapter 11

The Young Turks Continue

As the popularity of jazz increased on Indiana Avenue among the younger generation of jazz students, and word spread that one could receive an excellent jazz education, jam with established, seasoned jazz professionals and put a little money in their pockets, several youngsters descended on the Avenue to test their chops. One such jazz student was Ray Appleton.

Although an outsider and not a member of the Lockefield Gardens Housing Development jazz circle along with the Ridley brothers, Spaulding and Jones, Otis Ray Appleton gained the reputation of being a fantastic drummer. While auditioning for a chance to play at the Hub Bub, a local north side jazz spot, young Appleton appeared on stage one night and blew the audience away. A shocked bassist, Larry Ridley, approached him between sets and commented, "Man, you a little killer on those drums," hence the name Killer Ray. Otis Ray Appleton Jr. was born in Indianapolis on August 23, 1941, to Julia Griffin Appleton and Otis Ray Appleton Sr. Growing up in the Douglass Park area of the city, he, like many neighborhood kids, loved to play marbles. One day, Appleton was down on his knees shooting marbles with his friend Harold "Pee Wee" Williams when Williams suggested that they go downtown to the fire station, where the Drum and Bugle Corps practiced. When Appleton and Williams arrived, they witnessed a multitude of children frolicking in the building, playing various drums and bugles and generally making a lot of noise. As they approached this pandemonium, they observed an unoccupied drum set sitting idly in the corner. Williams prompted Appleton to go over and play the drums. Appleton complied.

After careful consideration, he slowly approached the drums, sat down, grabbed his sticks and began to pound a surprisingly synchronized, rhythmic drum pattern. So unique was his first venture with the drums that a fireman walked over and observed his performance. He said, "Kid, you've got some ability on those drums. Have you ever thought about playing in your school band? What school do you go to?" Appleton replied, "School 56 [Francis W. Parker]." The next week, the fireman called Larry Liggett, music instructor at the school, and Otis Appleton was invited to join the band. He was immediately assigned to the bass and snare drums, where he developed his love for music. The next year, his school band won a blue ribbon in the annual All-City Band Contest held at Arsenal Technical High School.

In 1958, Appleton entered Crispus Attucks High School and continued his music studies. He joined the band and developed a warm and respectful relationship with music teacher Russell Brown. Of Brown, he recalled, "Mr. Brown was very caring and concerned about me and all the music students who were there at that time." On weekends, he attended the music concerts held in Douglass Park, where he saw many of his neighborhood heroes, who were up-and-coming musicians, perform. During one unforgettable concert, he watched in amazement as Freddie Hubbard on trumpet and James Spaulding on tenor saxophone mounted the stage. They broke into some of the older jazz standards as Appleton listened attentively to the mixture of notes from both brass instruments. From that experience, he related, "My life was forever changed."

Appleton's uncle William Carruthers noticed that he had developed a deep appreciation for the drums, so one day, Carruthers purchased a high-quality drum set. When he presented the gift to his nephew, Appleton was thrilled beyond belief. He began to play the drums immediately, much to the displeasure of his mother. When his mother discovered who had purchased the drum set, she was not happy. Otis remembered, "My mother didn't speak to my uncle for two years after he bought me that drum set."

Appleton went to Indiana Avenue to observe the established musicians in order to sharpen his chops. One night, he witnessed the performance of drummer Paul Parker and began to make mental notes of his technique. He introduced himself to Parker and apprised him of his desire to play the drums, whereupon Parker took him under his wing. Parker also loaned him a pair of cymbals to complete Appleton's drum set. He became Appleton's primary jazz influence. Traveling up and down the Avenue and following Parker, his mentor, Appleton began to enter the jazz establishments at a young age. Once, he stopped by George's Bar to see the Paul Parker Trio, composed of Paul's brother, Buddy Parker, on saxophone and Harold Malone on piano. According to Appleton, club owner "Bob McClure kept an eagle eye on me to make sure I didn't drink alcohol."

After his tutorial sessions with Parker, Appleton got his first gig performing at the Brass Rail in downtown Indianapolis. There he performed with the baritone saxophonist Duke Hampton Trio, which included Harold Malone on piano. Later, as news of Appleton's musical ability traveled up and down the Avenue, he received an invitation to join trombonist Dave Baker's band, which included David Young on saxophone and Harold Gooch on Fender bass. They played six nights a week, earning ten dollars per night. Appleton's next stop was the Hub Bub Jazz Club, where he performed with Wes Montgomery on guitar and Melvin Rhyne on piano. Montgomery commented one night after a set, "Man you really can play!"

Phillip Arthur Ranelin, a jazz trombonist and contemporary of Appleton's who attended Arsenal Technical High School on the east side of Indianapolis, was born on May 25, 1939, to Kenneth Edwin Ranelin and Velader Vera Smith Ranelin in Indianapolis. The person with the most profound influence on his music career was his paternal grandmother, Helen Kimbrough Ranelin Crawford. She was the quintessential lover of fine music who enjoyed many of the jazz performances at the Sunset Terrace Ballroom. Often, she reminisced of her delight in seeing such jazz luminaries as tenor saxophonist Charlie Parker, bandleader and pianist Duke Ellington and Count Basie and trumpeters Dizzy Gillespie and Miles Davis perform live on stage. She possessed an extensive record collection that consisted of American music of various genres and exposed young Ranelin to the world of jazz at an early age. Undoubtedly, Ranelin developed an intense appreciation and deep respect for jazz and other forms of American music by witnessing the joy that it provided for his grandmother.

Ranelin's earliest music education was received at Hazel Hart Hendricks School 37, where he was initially and briefly instructed by Larry Liggett and then, for the remainder of his music education, by Reginald DuValle Jr. He felt very fortunate to have a music instructor whose specialty was his chosen instrument, the trombone. Recalling DuValle, Ranelin remembered, "As an instructor he was not intense…very laid back and a smart dresser, but he gave me a firm foundation on the instrument. It was a blessing having Mr. DuValle as my instructor."

As Ranelin's appreciation of jazz increased, the seeds of his desire to master the trombone slowly began to germinate. He enthusiastically anticipated the music instruction that he would receive in high school.

Phil Ranelin, a quiet but powerful trombonist who took his trade to the West Coast and dazzled fans there. He performed with Freddie Hubbard and was considered Hubbard's favorite trombonist.

Although Ranelin attended Arsenal Technical High School and participated in many facets of its music program, he was greatly indebted to Russell Brown of Crispus Attucks's music department for challenging him to be the best music student possible by giving him private instruction.

In 1952, while Ranelin was in grade school along with other aspiring music students, cognizant of its outstanding reputation in music instruction, he attended a summer session at Crispus Attucks High School with Russell Brown. "He was great…the ultimate educator, quite a performer with an advanced knowledge of music…He really could communicate with young people," Ranelin recalled. In 1957, Ranelin graduated from high school, and the following summer, he sought further music instruction from David Baker, who gave him private music lessons in his home. "He was very intense… very demanding and laid a lot of information on me," Ranelin noted.

In addition to this instruction, Ranelin briefly studied with the principal trombonist of the Indianapolis Symphony Orchestra at Butler University's Jordan Conservatory of Music.

Confident that his music instruction would provide him with a competitive edge on Indiana Avenue, in 1959 Ranelin joined the Renaud Jones Orchestra. He gained a considerable amount of performance experience from this group. As mentioned earlier, Jones was one of the original Brown Buddies who performed on Indiana Avenue in the late 1920s and early 1930s.

At the beginning of 1959, pianist/organist Melvin Rhyne, who was performing with guitarist Wes Montgomery at the popular Hub Bub Night Club, introduced Ranelin to Montgomery and encouraged him to seek an audition. Nervously, Ranelin sat in on a few performances. Montgomery liked his style and invited him to perform on other occasions. He comically recalled, "Man, when Melvin introduced me to Wes Montgomery, I was scared to death, but for me that was my beginning."

Ranelin continued to perform on the jazz circuit and appeared at the Place to Play, the British Lounge and the Club 13. During one performance at the Club 13, which was primarily a blues club, Ranelin was asked to try his hand playing the blues. Ranelin accepted the gig confident that his prior jazz music instruction would sustain him in making the transition from jazz to the blues. After the first set, which he put his heart and soul into, Ranelin said that somebody in the club shouted out, "Man, when yaw gonna play the blues?" Ranelin shook his head and chuckled.

In 1960, Ranelin relocated to Detroit to explore new horizons and face new challenges in the world of jazz. He became a fixture on the jazz circuit and appeared with various musicians in many of the city's jazz hot spots. He reunited with Earl Van Riper, pianist with the Wes Montgomery Trio, and bassist Mingo Jones, with whom he had previously performed in Indianapolis. He remained in Detroit for more than nine years.

In 1977, Ranelin moved to Los Angeles and immediately hooked up with trumpeter Freddie Hubbard, his music classmate from high school. Hubbard was receiving rave reviews in the world of jazz after recording his Grammy-winning album, *First Light*. Hubbard took Ranelin under his wing, and they performed with another Indianapolis jazz personality, bassist Kent Brinkley, at the popular Roxy nightclub located on the Sunset Strip.

He performed for many years in Los Angeles's hottest jazz nightspots and gained a solid reputation in the world of jazz. Ranelin also recorded many albums that were well regarded in jazz circles. In respect and admiration for his performing excellence, on November 11, 1999, Ranelin was designated by official resolution as a "Rare and Valuable Cultural Treasure" and as a "Cultural Ambassador throughout the Nation and to the World Audience" by the mayor and city council of Los Angeles. On November 11, 2001, he was also honored by United States congresswomen Maxine Waters and Juanita Millender-McDonald with certificates of appreciation for community service and excellence as an artist.

Several Indiana jazz entertainers cut their teeth on Indiana Avenue and carried their trade to the West Coast, such as guitarist Wes Montgomery, bassist Leroy Vinnegar, pianist Carl Perkins and drummer Willis Kirk. David Alexander Hardiman was born on June 15, 1938, to Nathan Clarence Hardiman and Sadie Frances Lyles Hardiman in Indianapolis. His parents were descendants of Indiana's Lyle's Station, an African American settlement founded in 1849 and located near Evansville. His mother was a self-taught pianist who also sang in the choir at the Eastern Star Baptist Church of Indianapolis.

Hardiman received his early music education at the McArthur Conservatory of Music, where he studied piano and had private trumpet lessons with educator/bandleader Lancaster Price. Later, he studied the piano and trumpet under the supervision of Ruth McArthur, Larry Leggett and James Compton at Francis W. Parker School 56 and John Hope School 26. In 1951, he entered Arsenal Technical High School and began music instruction under band director John White and orchestra director Walter Shaw. He played the trumpet in the band, orchestra and dance band. During this period, he met Cuban music instructor Juliano Juanzonez at the McArthur Conservatory of Music, who encouraged him to gather fellow music students and organize a band.

Shortly thereafter, the Monarchs were organized, which included James Spaulding on tenor saxophone, Melvin Rhyne and Al Walton on keyboards, Virgil Jones on trumpet and Eugene Manning on drums. Their popularity soared on Indiana Avenue, and they were contacted by the Walker Theatre entertainment manager, Matthew Dickerson, who frequently booked them to perform at the Walker Casino Ballroom. They also performed at many high school dances and music programs around the city.

During the summer of 1953, Hardiman took music courses at Crispus Attucks High School under the supervision of Russell Brown. He honed his music skills and met fellow students who had charted their courses in the world of music. Of Brown, he fondly remembered, "He was probably one of the most helpful and influential persons in helping a lot of the guys…he'd stay after class for hours, rehearsing you to make sure that you understood the lesson well…he was fantastic!"

In 1955, Hardiman went to Indiana University with the intent of majoring in music education and was a member of the Indiana University "Marching 100 Band" for four years. In his dormitory at East Hall, he met fellow music students who had been captivated by the young jazz artists of the day and who spent countless hours discussing the latest jazz records. Finally, the artistic urge became so unbearable that these musicians held jam sessions in their dormitories on the weekends to the delight of their fellow students.

Instantly, word of these impromptu and clandestine jazz sessions reached the office of Mr. Baines, dean of the School of Music. He was furious, summoned the guilty parties to his office and lined them up on the proverbial "red carpet." Baines lectured in great detail and impressed on them his opinion that jazz was not an academically accepted art form and that they should cease and desist from "playing that type of dreadful music immediately." The reprimanded students returned to their dormitories and continued to clandestinely play jazz in spite of Baines's dictum.

In 1959, after graduation, Hardiman obtained employment in the Indianapolis Public School system as a music instructor and taught at several elementary and junior high schools. After school, he found time to travel to Indiana Avenue and performed with the Eldridge Morrison and Jimmy Coe's Orchestras. Later, he organized the Original Chromatics Band, which included Aletra Hampton on piano, Bill Penick on saxophone, Everett Wade on bass and Sonny Williams on drums. Primarily, they performed for sorority and fraternity events, social clubs and teas. Later, guitarist Henry Gooch and his brother, Fender bassist Harold Gooch, joined this aggregation. Hardiman received his master's degree in music education from Butler University and was a member of the stage band at the Starlight Musical Concert series.

In 1971, Hardiman relocated to San Francisco and taught music at the Martin Luther King High School in Berkeley, California. He taught at the City College of San Francisco and Alameida and Contra Costa Community Colleges. Later, he performed in orchestras that accompanied international and national stars such as singers Johnny Ray, Tony Bennett, Peggy Lee and Nancy Wilson and bandleader Red Prysock. In 1978, his San Francisco All-Star Band released *It'll Be All Right*, which featured many of the jazz musicians in the San Francisco Bay area. In 1999, he returned to Indianapolis and was one of the premier performers at the inaugural Indy Jazz Festival. Hardiman retired from the City College of San Francisco after a forty-five-year teaching career.

Chapter 12

Al Coleman's British Lounge

The turbulent 1960s—characterized by tremendous sociopolitical upheaval across America with the assassinations of the Kennedys, Malcolm X and Martin Luther King; the mass demonstrations against an unpopular war in Vietnam; and the race riots from coast to coast—introduced a new chapter in the storied history of Indiana Avenue. As patrons left the Avenue in droves in search of new social experiences afforded by integration, the entertainment industry descended to the abyss of total destruction. Windows shuttered, doors closed and a sense of gloom permeated the atmosphere. Nonetheless, there were several "never-say-die" entrepreneurs and business owners determined to impede its march to the graveyard and return the Avenue to the perch of its former glory. One such establishment was the British Lounge.

Founded in 1943 as an entertainment establishment by Townsend Green, a former manager of the Walker Theatre, and his wife, Corina, it was ultimately purchased by entrepreneur/musician Albert Coleman in 1969. Coleman recognized the decline of the Avenue and dedicated his effort to continue live jazz entertainment and revive the dying industry. He related, "As soon as the ink dried on the contract, I immediately renovated the entire place and made it a class 'A' establishment." Being a member of the original Three Souls jazz trio, which had previously performed in entertainment venues on the Avenue, Coleman had a special sense of nostalgia for the glory days of jazz on the Avenue. The Three Souls trio had a very historically significant and interesting history.

Three Souls, a legendary group formed by Al Coleman that was widely sought all over town. All members had fantastic careers in business and education after music. *Courtesy of Indiana Historical Society.*

There were several surreal stories from Indiana Avenue during the early 1950s, wherein various musicians would inadvertently bump into one another in nightclubs, decide to perform together and then realize that their happenstance meeting may have been preordained. One such story belongs to the Three Souls. This trio was composed of Al Coleman on drums, Will Scott on bass and Henry D. Cain on piano. Al Coleman was born on August 18, 1927, in Indianapolis to Alvia and Helen Brown Coleman. His fondest recollection of his love for music as a child was his inexplicable fascination with the trombone. He desperately wanted to play the trombone, but being a tiny tot, his arms were too short to extend the trombone to the sixth position, so he chose an alternate instrument.

His father purchased a silver Bush 400 saxophone and encouraged Coleman to learn the basic rudiments of the instrument, but he did not enthusiastically follow the dictates of his father. Soon, he tired of this instrument and secretly sold it to neighborhood friend Jimmy Coe for five dollars! When his father discovered this clandestine transaction, young

Coleman had his britches warmed and was sent to bed without supper. As the story continues, bassist Will Scott and pianist Henry D. Cain played at Sea Ferguson's Cotton Club one night for the first time with other musicians and immediately noticed an indescribable chemistry that existed between their two instruments.

During intermission, the two huddled together and shared their feelings of amazement and vowed that they would launch out in a new and dynamic direction, but they knew that they required a master drummer to add to their group. For weeks, they traveled from nightclub to nightclub on and off Indiana Avenue and looked for that final "chemical" to be added to their "test tube."

On a rainy Saturday night, foot-tired and bone-weary from their travels around town, both men shuffled into the Udell Tavern and observed a young, bespectacled Al Coleman performing with guitarist Spec Maynard's band on stage. Both men recognized the precision of Coleman's drumsticks dancing on the leathery skin of his snare drum and the pristine sound of his cymbals and immediately knew that this was the drummer who could complement their instruments and advance their dream closer to reality. At intermission, they introduced themselves and invited Coleman to join the group, but initially he was a little apprehensive. They requested that he join them in rehearsal, to which Coleman emphatically responded, "Man, I got a gig here with this group, and I'm doing just fine."

After hours of discussion and arm twisting, Coleman finally agreed to attend a rehearsal at Cain's mother's house on Shriver Avenue. It was immediate chemistry. The Three Souls became popular while performing at the Cactus Club at Thirteenth and Northwestern Avenue. Many of the local sororities and fraternities booked them for engagements because their form of jazz was considered suave and sophisticated and appealed to the intellectual community.

On Indiana Avenue, they performed at the Cotton Club, P&P Club and the Place to Play, and as their popularity grew, they were signed by Bernie Herman of the Note Record Company and produced several hits that were very popular among the jazz community. If one were to microscopically examine the dynamics of the fraternal relationship between the Three Souls and their quest for success and excellence, one might discover an interesting phenomenon. From the beginning, all members demanded perfection and precision, and these elements were translated into their career goals in life.

Coleman owned six businesses, including a nightclub and vending machine company, and had more than fifty employees on his payroll. Four of his six businesses were directly related to jazz. Henry D. Cain moved to Las Vegas and performed with some of the world's greatest entertainers. Stars like singers Lola Falana, Nancy Wilson, Freida Payne and the Osmonds were backed up by Cain.

Scott embarked on a career in higher education and social work and attended Indiana University, where he received his bachelor's degree in 1963, his master's degree in 1964 and his doctorate in 1965. Scott spent more than five decades teaching at many of the prestigious historically black colleges and universities throughout the country. Among the awards and honors bestowed on him for his invaluable contributions to social work education are the Pioneer Award from the National Association of Social Workers, the Lifetime Achievement Award from the Council on Social Work Education and the Coastal Bend Lifetime Achievement Award. In addition, he received the Indiana University Alumni Lifetime Achievement Award. Three Souls performed together for more than fifty years until the death of Will Scott in 2004.

One of Al Coleman's fellow Crispus Attucks High School band mates trained by Russell Brown was fellow drummer Willis Kirk. Willis Franklin Kirk Jr. was born to Willis Franklin Kirk Sr. and Clara Bell Stevens Kirk on November 30, 1928, in Indianapolis, Indiana. He began his early music education studying percussion instruments at Hazel Hart Hendricks School 37 with music instructors Norman Merrifield and Russell Brown. His first music assignment occurred while in the classroom of Miss Stevens, who was a pianist. Kirk and his fellow music classmate Dickie Laswell were required to accompany Miss Stevens on playing marching music as students marched into the lunchroom at noontime and marched out of the school at the end of the day. He later attended John Hope School 26, reunited with Russell Brown and continued his education with percussion instruments.

In 1946, Kirk entered Crispus Attucks High School and joined the orchestra under the baton of LaVerne Newsome, played in the band directed by Russell Brown and sang in the choir under Miss Williams. As the "bebop craze" swept the country, Kirk could not resist the temptation to test his chops on Indiana Avenue. As a fourteen-year-old freshman, he traveled to the Avenue determined to win a chair in one of the popular jazz groups that performed there. Kirk painted a moustache with mascara on his top lip, lowered his voice a few octaves and entered the 440 Nightclub to seek a gig. He met with up-and-coming jazz guitarist Wes Montgomery and pianist Millard Lee. Later, he played with established musicians such as bandleader Dudley Storms, guitarist Henry Woods, trumpeter Roger Jones,

As a teenager, Willis Kirk performed with Duke Ellington and Charlie Parker by chance. He later taught music on a college level and became president of City College of San Francisco. *Courtesy of Willis Kirk.*

saxophonist Beryl Steiner, pianists Harold Malone and Purnell Coleman and bandleader/guitarist Clarence "Specs" Maynard.

In 1949, two events occurred that altered the course of Kirk's jazz career forever. One night, he went to the Sunset Terrace Ballroom to see the Duke Ellington Orchestra, but according to Kirk, unfortunately, Ellington's drummer, Sonny Greer, was so drunk that he literally fell off the bandstand into the crowd below. Ellington desperately needed a drummer because the show began in an hour.

Desperately, Ellington asked Kirk's friend Emmett Brown, a professional photographer, if he knew of anyone who could play the drums. Kirk stood next to Brown, and Brown pointed toward Kirk and said to Ellington, "This kid can play!" As trumpeter Ray Nance looked on, Ellington led young Kirk to the bandstand, sat him down behind the drums and pleaded, "Now kid, I want you to play."

A bewildered Kirk, with a lump in his throat, slowly joined in the music and finally caught his groove. He performed nonstop and enjoyed his instant celebrity. At the conclusion of the last set, Ellington smilingly shook his hand and commended him on a fine performance, but he did not pay him one red cent. Kirk was not disappointed and was just so happy to have performed with the Duke Ellington Orchestra.

A few months later, Kirk and his buddy Walter McCauley caught a cab and headed to the Sunset Terrace Ballroom, anxiously anticipating the performance of the saxophonist/bandleader Charlie Parker and his group, which featured trumpeter Miles Davis, drummer Max Roach, pianist Duke Jordan and bassist Tommie Potter. As they approached the door with five dollars in hand, someone hollered, "There he is, Bird [Charlie Parker]!" This stranger approached Willis and said, "Are you Kirk, man?" Kirk blinked and nodded in affirmation and thought to himself, "I don't know this man." Then, the stranger grabbed Kirk by the arm, led him to the bandstand and said, "Come on man, we gotta hit it at 9:00 and fill this contract!" He escorted Kirk on stage, sat him down behind the drums, went to the microphone and began to play. He then turned around and hollered, "Play boy, play!" and Kirk sat frozen in his seat. Kirk was petrified because he realized that the stranger who was hollering at him was actually Charlie "Yardbird" Parker!

After Kirk recovered from total shock and realized that he occupied Max Roach's chair, he played and kept time with the orchestra. At eleven o'clock sharp, the doors of the Sunset Terrace Ballroom swung open, and in walked Max Roach and Miles Davis. During intermission, Roach thanked Kirk for sitting in, but Miles Davis "looked at me as if I was dirt," Kirk remembered. "Charlie Parker called me off to the side and gave me ten dollars." "No, Mr. Parker," Kirk countered, but after three monetary refusals, Parker stuck the ten dollars in Kirk's pocket.

Kirk graduated from Butler University in 1956 after a 1953 tour with the Lionel Hampton Orchestra, during which he met and played with trumpeters Clifford Brown, Quincy Jones and Art Farmer; saxophonist Gi Gi Grice; vocalists Mel Torme, June Christy, Jackie Cain and Roy Krai; vibraphonist Peter Appleyard; and Fender bassist Monk Montgomery. He played at many venues in and around Indianapolis and taught instrumental music in the Indianapolis Public School system. He worked with many bands in various clubs on Indiana Avenue and performed at the Embers Nightclub.

Kirk received his master's degree in music education from Butler University in 1964 and his doctorate from Waldon University in 1975. He moved to San

Francisco, California, in 1968 and played on the entertainment circuit. He worked shows with vocalist Tony Bennett and Jon Hendricks and at the Ebony Fashion Fair and the Marines Memorial Theatre. He also recorded "It'll Be All Right" with the San Francisco All-Star Big Band, which featured saxophonist John Handy, guitarist Michael Howell and trombonist Tricky Lofton, under the leadership of Indianapolis native and trumpeter David Hardiman.

In 1981, Kirk traveled to Sao Paolo, Brazil, with Earl "Fatha" Hines, where Hines recorded his last album before his death. The following year, Kirk wrote an instructional book on brush playing on drums called *Brushfire*. He presented a workshop on his book in Sao Paulo in 1982. From 1969, Kirk was employed by City College of San Francisco and became president of the college in his last two years before retirement in 1991. During his tenure in San Francisco, Kirk served as vice-president of the San Francisco Arts Commission and served two four-year terms. He also served on the board of the Friends and Foundation of the San Francisco Public Library and served as secretary for one term.

Kirk composed and conducted a jazz oratorio entitled *Rejoice! Rejoice!*, which was a one-and-a-half-hour production that featured a fifty-voice choir and ten musicians. It was performed before the International Association of Jazz Educators Convention in New York City and Long Beach, California, in 2002 and 2003 and was recorded in Indianapolis in 2004. Kirk has been active in the San Francisco Bay–area arts community and served on a panel to discuss the history of jazz and art in America. Kirk is currently writing music for various groups and ensembles.

One of Willis Kirk's early schoolmates/band mates who jammed with him in the dimly lit jazz spots on Indiana Avenue was Carl Perkins. Perkins was born on August 16, 1928, to Edward and Bessie Lagrone Hudson-Perkins in Indianapolis. He was the fourth of thirteen children in a family that struggled economically during the Great Depression. Perkins was exposed to classical and jazz music around the house and tinkered on his family's Steinway piano as he entertained his siblings on many occasions.

His younger brother Frederick recalled a childhood story that he fondly remembered and cherished. "One time, the dead of winter, wind howling outside of the old house, nothing going over the old coal burning stove and we were all quiet. All of a sudden, Carl started striking chords and we said, 'Hey that's pretty good, do that again!' Everybody paid attention and got around the piano, and he went from there. He kept on practicing and practicing and got better and better. He never got a real piano music lesson 'cause we didn't have the money…he just sort of picked it up on his own."

The Perkins siblings giggled at Carl's playing style because it was unique and nontraditional. His trademark was playing the piano with his left hand in a ninety-degree angle to the keyboard and using his elbow to play bass notes.

Perkins commented on his unusual playing style: "When I was small, my hand was too little to make the bass chords so I turned my hand around and used my elbow to make them." Childhood friends Norma Martin-Cork and Harold Andrews comically remembered Perkins playing the piano. Martin-Cork remembered, "He loved to play for us children in the recreation room in the basement of the Lockefield Gardens Housing Development. One

Carl Perkins, a jazz giant whom Miles Davis regarded as his favorite pianist. He died at an all-too-early age, and his recordings are still collectors' gold. *Courtesy of Raii Jordan.*

day, he played for us dressed up like Superman with a big red *S* mounted on a yellow diamond-shaped background emblazoned on his shiny, dark-blue, long-sleeved shirt and red cape draped around his neck. We all started laughing, and Carl just loved it!"

Although the Perkins family was very religious and attended the Apostolic Church, his parents did not discourage his desire to play the piano.

Perkins attended Crispus Attucks High School and took courses in the music department with Russell Brown, Norman Merrifield and LaVerne Newsome. Initially, he studied the clarinet with Brown, but he soon tired of the instrument and returned to his first love, the piano. Occasionally, he played at after-school dances with fellow schoolmates bassist Leroy Vinnegar and drummer Carroll Engs. After graduation, Perkins journeyed to Indiana Avenue and became a member of the house band at the popular Henri's Nightclub.

During his tenure there, a dispute arose between Perkins and nationally known jazz pianist Erroll Garner that grew out of Perkins's playing style. Garner accused Perkins of imitating his playing style, and Perkins countered and said that he had been playing this style before he even knew about Erroll Garner. He disregarded Garner's admonitions and continued to play according to his unique style.

In 1948, Perkins left Indianapolis with the immensely popular rhythm-and-blues bandleader Paul "Hucklebuck" Williams, whose hit record "Do the Hucklebuck" sparked a dance craze that swept across the country. Perkins accompanied Williams and his orchestra to Hollywood and performed at the Sherry's nightspot on the Sunset Strip. Later, he met song stylist Dinah Washington, who appeared in the hottest jazz clubs in Hollywood, and briefly played in her orchestra. Washington was so impressed with Perkins's mastery of the jazz piano that she literally begged him to play in her orchestra.

As word of Perkins's musical ability circulated around Hollywood, he was sought by the crème de la crème of the entertainment industry. He performed with trumpeters Dizzy Gillespie, Miles Davis (who commented that Perkins was the greatest jazz pianist with whom he had ever performed) and Clifford Brown; drummers Max Roach and Illinois Jacquet; saxophonists Dexter Gordon and Frank Morgan; and violinist Hezekiah Leroy Gordon "Stuff" Smith. Perkins died on March 17, 1958, in Los Angeles.

In the 1950s, drummer Willis Kirk, guitarist Wes Montgomery, pianist/vibraphonist Buddy Montgomery, Fender bassist Monk Montgomery and Lucy Johnson played at many of the entertainment clubs on and off Indiana Avenue. Although Johnson assumed the name Debbie Andrews, a name more appealing to the entertainment industry, she was affectionately named "the Little Hen" by her adoring band mates.

Debbie Andrews was born Lucy Johnson to Willie and Eleanor Whitehead Johnson on October 13, 1927, in Rome, Georgia. After relocating to Indianapolis as a youth, Andrews sang in several church choirs, developed a love for music and soon discovered that she was blessed with a beautiful voice. In her teenage years, she transitioned from the sanctimonious sound of the church choir to the hot and spicy tunes of jazz and popular music and blazed a trail directly to the jazz clubs on Indiana Avenue. Her brother, Sonny Johnson, drummer with the Montgomery-Johnson Quintet, took her under his wing, and Andrews performed with his group in many of the jazz nightclubs along Indiana Avenue.

Although her debut into the world of jazz occurred at the Flame Show Bar in Detroit, her big break in show business occurred when she was discovered by orchestra leader Duke Ellington while performing in a nightclub in St. Louis, Missouri. Commenting on the musical genius of Debbie Andrews, Duke Ellington related, "She has the type of voice that I've been searching for ever since Ivy Anderson retired from show business." In her first appearance with the Ellington Orchestra, she received thunderous applause for her rendition of "Lover Come Back to Me." She toured with Ellington for several years and signed a contract with Mercury Records in 1952 after performing "September Song" with the Ellington Orchestra on the live broadcast over the

Debbie Andrews (Lucy Johnson), sister of drummer Sonny Johnson, was discovered by Duke Ellington. *Courtesy of Beverly Johnson.*

Mutual Network of the *Concert at Midnight from Carnegie Hall*. In April 1952, she performed in the first radio broadcast from John Dolphin's record shop in Hollywood with disc jockey Tony Vance. Early in 1953, she performed in a big celebration for Red Saunders's fifty-year anniversary as musical director of Club DeLisa. Andrews placed third in the *Pittsburgh Courier*'s poll of female vocalists and performed in that organization's *Operation Music* concert of poll winners later that year. She later recorded with United Records, and her first release garnered the attention of *Down Beat* magazine, which ran a sterling review in its rhythm-and-blues section on March 25, 1953. She died on March 27, 1987, in Pasadena, California.

Debbie Andrews's brother, affectionately known as "Sonny," was a member of the Montgomery-Johnson Quintet that included guitarist Wes Montgomery, pianist/vibraphonist Buddy Montgomery, Fender bassist Monk Montgomery and tenor saxophonist Alonzo "Pookie" Johnson. Robert Lee "Sonny" Johnson was born on November 9, 1930, to Willie Lee Johnson and Eleanor Whitehead Johnson in Rome, Georgia. In his early years, his family relocated to Indianapolis, where he attended Crispus Attucks High School and developed a desire to play the drums. His intensity and determination were immediately recognized by band director Russell Brown as Johnson spent many hours after school practicing his craft. He played in the school's band and orchestra and also performed with various neighborhood groups at parties and sock hops around the city.

His professional career began on Indiana Avenue; at the age of sixteen, he performed with guitarist Wes Montgomery, pianist/vibraphonist Buddy Montgomery, Fender bassist Monk Montgomery and saxophonist Alonzo "Pookie" Johnson at Sea Ferguson's Cotton Club in 1946. Later, this group formed the Montgomery-Johnson Quintet and made history by being the first African American jazz group to perform on local television. In 1951, his group backed vocalist Flo Garvin on her program *Sentimental Journey*, which aired on WFBM television station 6.

Johnson made several recordings with Wes Montgomery, including *The Montgomery Brothers and Five Others* and *Various Instrumentalists Almost Forgotten*. He traveled to New York to join the Art Farmer Orchestra and recorded *The Work of Art* and *The Art Farmer Septet*. Johnson performed with many musical groups at the leading nightclubs on Indiana Avenue, namely the Cotton Club, George's Bar, Henri's, P&P Club, the British Lounge and other hot spots. He later performed with jazz organist Jimmy Smith, trumpeter/conductor/arranger Quincy Jones, pianist/composer/bandleader Herbie Hancock and rhythm-and-blues singer Norman Connors. One of his most enjoyable Indiana Avenue experiences was performing with the Hampton Family Band, which included his great friend, trombonist Locksley "Slide" Hampton. Robert "Sonny" Johnson died on July 14, 2001, and as per his request, his remains were shipped to Africa and buried in the Motherland.

For several years, Kirk was employed as a music instructor in the Indianapolis Public School system and worked with two prominent musicians/music educators, Larry Liggett and Lancaster Price, who later made names for themselves on and off Indiana Avenue. Laurence Leonard Leggett was born on October 23, 1921, to Joseph Hardy Leggett and Mary Elizabeth Branch Leggett in Brazil, Indiana. Both parents were natives of Mississippi who had relocated to Brazil in the early twentieth century. His maternal grandfather, Reverend John Henry Branch, was a Baptist minister who was called to the pulpit of the Second Baptist Church in Brazil when his mother was twelve years old. His father was a graduate of Tuskegee Institute, Tuskegee, Alabama, who had majored in chemistry and was a student in its glazier division.

His father's research interest was inorganic chemistry and soil science, and he specialized in the production of inorganic elements to produce bricks. He sought employment in Brazil as an industrial chemist in its manufacturing division and submitted his credentials to the Brazil Brick Company, where they were scrutinized and accepted and an employment offer was made. As the company eagerly awaited the arrival of its newly hired chemist, it was shocked to discover that he was an African American.

Immediately, the company rescinded the employment offer, with the explanation that an African American could not be employed on equal footing with a white man for fear that it would be detrimental to the harmony of the company. Joseph Leggett had exhausted his finances and did not have train fare to return to Tuskegee; therefore, he had to accept a janitorial position with the company, to his dismay. He then met Mary Elizabeth Branch at the Second Baptist Church, fell in love, married and began a family.

Laurence (Larry) Leggett was raised in a home environment that celebrated fine music. His grandfather, Reverend Branch, played the clarinet, and music was an integral part of his family's daily activities. One day, little Larry played with toys in his room while his father did chores around the house. Temporarily distracted, his father left the room to attend to a concern and realized that a clarinet was seemingly being played by itself in Larry's room. Quickly returning to the room to investigate, to his amazement he witnessed his little four-year-old son clutching the barrel of the clarinet with his tiny fingers and blowing full notes. As he stood in the doorway in total disbelief, he realized that his son was musically gifted, and he then decided to encourage him to study music. His grandfather, Reverend Branch, realized that young Larry possessed a beautiful singing voice and often would permit him to sing during his church services.

A musically gifted young achiever, Leggett entered grammar school and was one of a few African Americans in the entire school; however, that factor did not deter him from excelling academically, musically, athletically and in the classroom. His musical gift was immediately recognized by a kind and caring teacher, Robert Ernhart, who took him under his wing and nurtured his music development. Under Ernhart's tutelage, Leggett earned the distinction of being the youngest member of the Brazil High School Marching Band, participating from the age of ten years until his graduation.

He was an all-American class clarinetist while in high school, found time to play varsity football and semiprofessional baseball and won Wabash Valley Conference and All-State honors in high school football. He began to play music professionally at the age of thirteen as local musicians recognized his aptitude for jazz improvisation and ability to read music very well. He performed with various jazz and popular music groups and performed in neighboring cities in Indiana and Illinois. Later, he organized his own jazz band called the Dukes, which was very popular among the jazz listeners in Clay County, and produced a record on a cardboard format. The record contained two songs, "I'll Never Smile Again" and "Boogit."

He entered Indiana State Teachers College, where he earned a Bachelor of Science and a Master of Science degree in music education and was the first African American member of the Symphonic Orchestra and the Marching Sycamores Band. More importantly, he was the first in the one-hundred-hour music degree program.

In 1948, Leggett was hired as an instrumental music teacher for the Indianapolis Public School system and was assigned to Crispus Attucks High

Larry Liggett, bandleader and educator who mentored many of the up-and-coming musicians of the Avenue. He was the first African American to march in his college (Indiana State College) marching band. *Courtesy of Valerie Leggett-Davidson.*

School and fourteen other African American elementary schools. His career as a professional musician developed rapidly during the 1950s, as rock-and-roll emerged from the classic sounds of rhythm and blues. Leggett and his popular combo, Three Flips and a Flop, became the toast of the town of the Indianapolis nightclub scene and among the Indy 500 racing elite. They enjoyed a multiyear engagement at Mates' White Front Nightclub, the official nightspot of the Indy 500 drivers, crew and fans.

In 1954, Phil and Leonard Chess, owners of Chess Record Company, Chicago, Illinois, signed Leggett to a three-year contract under the name "Larry Liggett."

His first single, "Perdido Mambo," attracted national attention and earned him a New Artist citation in the prestigious *Down Beat* magazine. After completing national tours while recording on the Chess label, he opted to localize his professional career and declined offers to tour internationally with the bands of his mentors, bandleaders Duke Ellington and Count Basie.

In 1957, he organized the Larry Liggett Orchestra, with personnel consisting of lifelong music educators and professional musicians of the Indianapolis Public School system. His orchestra earned the enviable distinction of being the first African American group to enter into a multiyear contract with major Indianapolis venues, breaking the color line at the exclusive Marriott Hotel. He later performed at the Stouffer's Inn-Meridian and remained there for seven years. In 1969, his orchestra released its first album, entitled *Larry Liggett Swings at Stouffer's*.

Liggett earned national and international recognition as a jazz musician and scholar of music education and ethnomusicology and was a guest lecturer and performer at many colleges and universities. As a teacher and conductor, he compiled an outstanding record of participation in the annual statewide Indiana School of Music Association music contest, with fifty-eight winning bands and orchestras in thirty years of classroom instruction.

In December 1991, he was awarded the highest civilian honor in the state of Indiana, the distinguished Sagamore of the Wabash, and eight years later, he was awarded the Governor's Arts Award. Laurence Leonard Leggett passed away on January 20, 2001, in Indianapolis, Indiana. The little four-year-old toddler who grasped his father's clarinet with his tiny hands and began to play many years ago had blazed a celestial path across the musical heavens and had etched his name on the stars.

Lancaster (Lanny) Warren Price was born on March 9, 1924, to John Morgan Price and Pearl Venetta Fields Price in the tiny coal mining town of Montgomery, West Virginia. His mother was a major influence in his

Lancaster Price, a Montford Point Marine, performed with the Larry Liggett Orchestra and taught in the Indianapolis Public School system. *Courtesy of Indiana Historical Society.*

early years and was reputed to be an excellent vocalist at the family's church. Price attended Simmons High School and received his early music instruction from Solomon Phillips. He recalled Phillips as being a very demanding and dedicated music teacher.

Price was a member of the all-black Montford Point Marines, a group that was stationed in the South Pacific during World War II. As a member of the Special Service Marine Band, his duty was to entertain troops throughout the islands. He was honorably discharged in 1946 and came to Indianapolis to further his education. He was introduced to Ruth McArthur, music supervisor of the Indianapolis Public School system. McArthur had recently opened a conservatory of music, and she convinced him to bring his first music student, David Hardiman, to the conservatory for instruction. After observing his teaching techniques and assessing his knowledge of music theory, she hired him on a full-time basis.

Price was offered an opportunity to work in the Midwest in the early 1950s; therefore, he relocated his wife, Ida, and daughter, Ellen, to Jefferson City, Missouri. He accepted a teaching position in the music department at Lincoln University, where he taught for three years. Upon returning to Indianapolis, Price performed on trumpet, flute, saxophone and upright bass with the most popular musical groups along Indiana Avenue. This lineup included saxophonist Jimmy Coe, pianist Jimmy McDaniels, trombonists Eldrige Morrison and Reginald DuValle and bassist Leroy Vinnegar.

In the mid-1950s, he toured with the Tiny Bradshaw Orchestra throughout the country and then toured with guitarist Floyd Smith, who had recently left Andy Kirk and the Clouds of Joy Orchestra. During this period, Price organized a musical group called the Lanny Lancaster Trio.

This group consisted of Price on trumpet, Maurice Johnson on piano and Oliver "Cokey" Napier on drums. The trio frequently performed nightly at the Brass Rail Nightclub on Ohio Street in downtown Indianapolis.

Price often played with the Larry Liggett Big Jazz Band. After Liggett's death, he led the remaining band members in several concerts in tribute to Liggett. During the day, he taught music education in the Indianapolis Public School system and at night was a graduate student in music education. In 1971, he received his master's degree in music education from Butler University.

Willis Kirk often performed on Indiana Avenue with an entertainer who was a showman as well as a musician. He commanded the attention of every patron in the venues by way of his zany routines on and off stage. Kirk recounted, "Sy Jones got gigs at the Industrial Club, and everybody liked him…he'd lay on the floor or bar on his back and play his horn, and folks would fall out [laughing]. He was the ultimate showman, and he'd steal the show!"

Sy Jones was born on November 23, 1923, to James Nathaniel and Mattie Puckett Jones in Indianapolis. He sang in the children's choir and was a member of a gospel quartet at Caldwell Chapel AME Church, where he developed a love of music. He entered Crispus Attucks High School in 1937, began his music education under the direction of Russell Brown, Norman Merrifield and LaVerne Newsome and played in the school band and orchestra. His first instrument was the clarinet; he soon tired of the sound and opted to play the saxophone, but he could not afford to purchase it. Jones wanted it so badly that he obtained a job solely for the objective of earning money so that he could purchase a Selma Bear saxophone.

After high school graduation, he enrolled at Virginia State College, Petersburg, Virginia, at his parents' insistence that he prepare himself for a career in law, but he had other ideas. Jones pursued his prelaw curriculum but still found time to play in venues around the college town. In the midst of his college career, he was called to service in the United States Army during World War II. After his honorable discharge, he went to New York and played in the Harlem nightclub circuit for seven months and then returned to Indianapolis and performed at the Sunset, Cactus Club, Henri's, P&P Club and other jazz clubs on and off Indiana Avenue.

Jones traveled to Louisville, Kentucky, with guitarist Wes Montgomery and organist/bandleader Jack McDuff, and during this stint, he auditioned for the Lionel Hampton Orchestra and won a seat in the brass section. He performed with Hampton for five years; however, the last two years were on an intermittent basis as Hampton's wife had the reputation of being a disruptive force and alienated many musicians in the orchestra. Issues of pay and performance scheduling were her main points of contention.

One day, she confronted Jones concerning rumors that he allegedly had spread about her alleged extramarital affairs with fellow band mates, which he vehemently denied. On the spot, she fired Jones, but Hampton quickly called him back. Jones returned to Indianapolis and performed with local musicians such as guitarist Wes Montgomery, saxophonists Pookie Johnson and Jimmy Coe, bassist Leroy Vinnegar and pianists Carl Perkins and Erroll Grandy. He received the nickname "Floor Show" for his zany antics on stage. Near the end of his career, he received a request to perform at the plush Franklin Country Club for a short stint and performed there for twelve years. Sy "Floor Show" Jones died on September 24, 2004, in Indianapolis, Indiana.

Willis Kirk received his early music education at George Washington Carver School 87 with another interesting musician noted for his zany antics. According to Kirk, "On the way to Crispus Attucks High School, Russell Webster got on the streetcar each day, and starting from the top of the hill to the bottom, he'd entertain the passengers whether they wanted to be entertained or not with his saxophone. Everybody got a kick out of that!"

Russell Webster, the youngest of twelve children of William and Clotelle Webster, was born on April 10, 1928, in Indianapolis. A devout Methodist and homemaker, Clotelle was the organist for a local Baptist church in their east side neighborhood. As a child, Webster accompanied his mother to church and helped her push the heavy pedals of the church's pipe organ during services. His mother insisted that all of her children learn to play the piano, as well as any other instrument that they would endeavor to learn, and Webster received her most intensive instruction; he was also encouraged to pursue multiple woodwinds instruction at the Arthur Jordan Conservatory of Music (Butler University) under the careful tutelage of Charles Henzie. Webster performed with the Indianapolis Symphony Orchestra under the direction of conductor Fabien Sevitzky in an exchange program with students of the conservatory.

He received musical instruction at Crispus Attucks High School under Russell Brown and LaVerne Newsome, and although a serious student, Webster was known to test the boundaries of authority and to have fun with other classmates. Comically, he recalled the times that he and best friends, saxophonist Alonzo "Pookie" Johnson and trombonist Reginald DuValle, ignored the instructions of their teachers, sneaked back into the

Russell Webster, a saxophonist who was known as the "Whistling Postman." He performed all around Indianapolis. He was a sideman on the recording of the LP *Dr. Funkenstein*, which is an Indianapolis classic.

music rooms at Crispus Attucks and experimented with jazz, playing the latest tunes. Upon hearing the commotion, the custodians rushed into the room and demanded that the students leave the room. "We were afraid that they'd tell Russell Brown and get us in trouble, but they never did," recounted Webster.

Later, Webster developed his sound with other aspiring musicians who yearned to showcase their talents, and although a minor, he was a frequent late-night visitor to the dinner clubs and speakeasies on Indiana Avenue. With a moustache freshly painted on his upper lip and horn in hand, he followed the footsteps of his older brother, Archie, a talented trumpet player. He waited patiently for a chance to sit in with established musicians like pianist Erroll Grandy and bassist Leroy Vinnegar or the chance meeting with legendary talents traveling through town, such as bandleaders Duke Ellington and Cab Calloway.

In 1946, Webster served in the 384th Regiment Army Band, which garnered him much praise, and participated in USO performances with Terre Haute native, pianist/arranger/composer and bandleader Claude Thornhill and comedian/actor/musician Jackie Gleason. The highlights of his career included a jazz exhibition in the royal palace of the Crown Prince of Siam (now Thailand).

Upon his return to Indianapolis in 1952, he and Alonzo "Pookie" Johnson assumed their roles as the brash new mavericks and shaped the emerging sounds of jazz on Indiana Avenue. They teamed up with fellow Indiana Jazz Foundation Hall of Fame recipients guitarist Wes Montgomery; saxophonists Jimmy Coe and David Young; trombonists J.J. Johnson, Locksley Slide Hampton and Reginald DuValle; bassists Monk Montgomery and Mingo Jones; pianist Buddy Montgomery; pianist/organist Melvin Rhyne; and drummer Willis Kirk.

Webster was recognized as one of Indianapolis's most celebrated jazz performers, a classically trained virtuoso known as a leading saxophone player and prolific jazz composer. He composed music for Jimmy Coe's Orchestra and was a front man for the live ensemble performances. In 1988, the Russell Webster Quartet was chosen to perform in a joint concert called *Calypso and Jazz*, commemorating the Tenth Pan-American Games. Webster received international exposure when he appeared as a guest soloist with acclaimed recording artist Michael McDonald in Indianapolis in 2001 and performed for former president Jimmy Carter and Habitat for Humanity–International's twenty-fifth anniversary celebration. It was televised worldwide, live from Conseco fieldhouse. Russell Webster died on September 8, 2007.

Willis Kirk related that although many of the jazz groups were popular on the Avenue, there were several entertainers who performed solo. One such entertainer was Willis Dyer.

Willis Dyer was born on May 31, 1918, to Willis B. and Elizabeth O'Neal Dyer in Nashville, Tennessee. He was better known as "Mr. Hammond Organ" and was one of the first jazz musicians in Indianapolis to sport a

Hammond organ with all the accessories. Dyer began his music career in the early 1930s and played with bandleaders Jimmy Nicks and later with Frank Reynolds and his 15 Kings of Swing. Dyer performed with the Dudley Storms Orchestra at the Sunset Terrace Ballroom, the Walker Ballroom and the Sunset Terrace Ballroom, as well as at the Knights of Columbus Hall on Indiana Avenue.

In the late 1940s, Dyer organized his own group on the bandstand at the P&P Nightclub on Indiana Avenue that featured "Stuff" Watson on bass. After leaving the P&P Club, he formed a partnership with Will Scott, and this duo was known as the Will and Will Combo. They performed at the Cotton Club, Tropic, Thunderbird and Cactus Club.

Chapter 13
Local Musicians Hop on the Bandwagon

An interesting twist to the musical legacy of Crispus Attucks High School was the fact that one of its faculty members who did not teach music performed on Indiana Avenue for many years. Carl Wendell Hines Jr., the son of Carl Wendell Sr. and Ruth Johnson Hines, was born on September 1, 1940, in Wilson, North Carolina. His father was a self-taught musician who played in the band and graduated from North Carolina A&T University. Later, Hines Sr. was employed as a mathematics teacher and band director at the Charles H. Darden High School in Wilson, North Carolina. When Carl Jr. was a youngster, he and his father entertained themselves at home by listening to the radio. His father enjoyed big-band music by Duke Ellington, Count Basie and Jimmy Lunceford and popular music by Rosemary Clooney and Patti Page.

In his early years, Carl Jr. listened to the rhythm-and-blues music programs broadcast from Randy's Record Shop of Gallatin, Tennessee, on the WLAC radio station. He enjoyed the sounds of Little Richard, the Drifters with Clyde McPhatter, James Brown and Ruth Brown. At fifteen years of age, his life and musical taste changed forever. One night, he was listening to the popular local African American radio program *Sepia Serenade*, which featured all kinds of black music, when the disc jockey played trumpeter Clifford Brown and drummer Max Roach's recording of the popular jazz tune "Cherokee." According to Carl, "Man, that record blew my mind! I was determined to learn as much as I could about this kind of music." That Christmas, he received a piano, and that intensified his desire to play jazz music. He taught himself to play jazz tunes by listening to records by Charlie Parker, Miles Davis and J.J. Johnson. He also searched all around town for someone to teach him how to play jazz but found no one.

In the fall of 1957, Hines entered Tennessee State Agricultural and Industrial University in Nashville, and following in his father's footsteps, he majored in mathematics in the hopes of becoming an educator. In college, he met a group of outstanding jazz musicians on campus and in the city. These musicians inspired him to continue his study of jazz by introducing him to new music and sharpening his technical skills. He graduated in 1962; four years later, he earned his master's degree in mathematics at the University of Tennessee–Knoxville.

Hines taught for a year in Alcoa, Tennessee, and then went to New York City to explore the excitement of the jazz scene; he sought employment to sustain himself by washing dishes and doing other odd jobs. His undergraduate college roommate, Milton Baltimore, convinced him to come to Indianapolis, where he might find employment. He followed Baltimore's advice and in 1964 landed a teaching position in Crispus Attucks's mathematics department.

While he was teaching math, Hines ventured onto Indiana Avenue and became a part of the local jazz scene. As news of his musical ability spread, he got gigs with established jazz men like Jimmy Coe, Alonzo "Pookie" Johnson, Dudley Storms and Lavon Kemp. His first professional engagement was with the Chromatics, which included Bill Penick on tenor saxophone, David Hardiman on trumpet, Everett Wade on bass, Henry Gooch on guitar and Larry Clark Sr. on drums. He also jammed with Clem Tiggs on drums and Tiny Adams on bass at Al Coleman's British Lounge and the new Sunset Club, and he played with the Larry Liggett Band for more than fifteen years. Other groups that he performed with included Al Finnell and the Mastertones and Hazel Johnson and Famili.

Hines's love for jazz took an artistically creative departure from performing to a literary expression. In 1962, his work "Two Jazz Poems" was published in *American Negro Poetry*, compiled by Arna Bontemps. That poem has been reprinted in more than seventy-five books and translated into a number of other languages. In 1968, the day after Dr. Martin Luther King Jr. was assassinated, Hines wrote a poem dedicated to King's memory entitled "Now that He Is Safely Dead." It was included in the recorded song cycle *Through This Vale of Tears*, a tribute to and commentary on King by David Baker, chair of the jazz department at the Indiana University School of Music.

Another jazz fixture on Indiana Avenue with a nonmusical connection to Crispus Attucks High School was Mary Moss. She was employed by the

Mary Moss came to Indianapolis with her husband as "King & Mary" and performed at many of the newly integrated clubs off Indiana Avenue. *Courtesy of Larry Goshen.*

school for a few years in the main office as an administrative assistant to the principal. Moss was born in Kentucky and attended high school in Louisville. Later, she attended Kentucky State College, Frankfort, where she sang with the university choir, which traveled throughout the South performing at historically black colleges and universities.

Moss relocated to Indianapolis in 1958 and immediately joined the ranks of the entertainment community. She married King Moss and toured with her husband as King & Mary, appearing in many of the exclusive nightclubs in

Canada such as the Chans Lounge in Winnipeg. Moss also appeared for two years at the Thunderbird Lounge in Indianapolis with owner and vocalist Boyd Bennett, who had the 1950s rhythm-and-blues hit "Seventeen," and bandleader Jimmy McDaniels. She also performed at LaRue's Supper Club in Indianapolis for seven years, backed by the Jimmy Coe Quintet. Later, she sang for larger and more appreciative audiences at the Crown Room, the Embers, the Pink Poodle and the Town and Country Lounge, all located in Indianapolis.

In the early 1970s, Moss appeared on television channel 13 daily with George Willeford, host of the live morning music and variety show and chairman of the Butler University drama department, and then moved to channels 4 and 8 as both a performer and a commentator, discussing the many aspects of show business. During the course of her career, she performed with such entertainers as Dick Gregory, Rowan & Martin, Dinah Washington, Brook Benton, Jerry Van Dyke and Hank Marr. In 2000, she founded the jazz presentation *Women Simply Kickin' It*, which provided a showcase for the talents of twenty female entertainers and singers. In the 1990s and early 2000s, Moss became more deeply involved with her church, Ebenezer Baptist, and ended her entertainment career.

Some jazz historians have chuckled over the years and stated that perhaps jazz ability may be transferred from generation to generation via a person's DNA. The Montgomery brothers are a case in point—Wes, Buddy and Monk were siblings and jazz giants on their respective instruments. Another Indiana Avenue jazz artist who could boast an outstanding music pedigree was Clifford Aaron Ratliff, a descendant of Noble Sissle, the early twentieth-century multitalented musician.

Clifford Aaron Ratliff was born on June 29, 1947, to James and Sadie Cissell Ratliff in Indianapolis. One of nine children, he was raised in a musical environment where every family member played an instrument. Their family was one of few in the neighborhood that had a piano. Ratliff sat for many hours practicing classical music standards that were routinely played at home by his mother. His mother was a cousin of singer, songwriter, bandleader and composer Noble Sissle, who teamed with Eubie Blake to create *Shuffle Along* in 1921. *Shuffle Along* was the first all-black Broadway musical to become a box office hit on the Great White Way, the nickname for a section of Broadway in the Midtown section of New York that encompasses the theater district between Forty-second and Fifty-third Streets. Ratliff's great-uncles Aaron and George Dimmitt were accomplished trumpet players well known for their musical abilities in Indianapolis entertainment circles.

Cliff Ratliff, a trumpeter who was tutored by Russell Brown and performed with many groups along the Avenue. *Courtesy of Clifford Ratliff.*

Ratliff attended Public School 23, where he was taught by Reginald DuValle Jr., Willis Kirk and Al Officer. At home, he played the piano but slowly developed a fondness for the trumpet. In 1961, he studied under Crispus Attucks High School's Russell Brown and joined the school band, orchestra and choir. Ratliff was profoundly affected by the concern and dedication of Russell Brown. He related that on many occasions Brown would remain after school for hours instructing band students on the finer points of music theory. Also, Ratliff remembered the band's participation in the Butler University Bowl, where students from throughout the city convened at the university for a music competition. Afterward, Brown's students were invited to his home for food and entertainment. Ratliff recalled, "He'd tell us students to testify, which meant to explore the limits of our artistic abilities." Brown would play the latest jazz or popular music recording and let each student improvise on his instrument.

During this period, Ratliff developed an intense desire to test his chops on Indiana Avenue. On many occasions, he told his parents that he was arriving home late at night because he had attended a house party or dance. Unbeknownst to his parents, who sternly forbade his presence on Indiana Avenue, Ratliff hid his trumpet in the coal shed, returned to retrieve it and headed directly to the Sunset Terrace Ballroom on the Avenue. He could perform only until 10:30 p.m. because his curfew required him to be in bed by 11:00 p.m. He comically reminisced, "Had my parents known that I was playing at the Sunset, they'd have killed me!" Ratliff had the enviable distinction of performing with one of Motown's seminal groups, Junior Walker and the All-Stars, led by the soulfully sweet saxophonist and vocalist Autry DeWalt Mixon Jr. Ratliff sat in with the group on several performances in Indianapolis when it was touring the country with its mega-hits, "Shot Gun," "Do the Boomerang," "I'm a Road Runner" and "Shake and Finger Pop."

Ratliff entered the United States Air Force in 1970 and was stationed stateside in Columbus, Mississippi, and abroad in Okinawa, Japan. While in Japan, he was a member of the air force band that backed a touring pianist, the legendary Mary Lou Williams, and Ike Cole, brother of popular music legend Nat King Cole.

Ratliff entered Indiana State University in 1971 with the objective of pursuing a career in music instruction, but his longing to be home on the weekends jamming with his friends on Indiana Avenue quickly disrupted his academic pursuit. "I'd spend more time at home than I did in the classroom," he humorously remembered. In Indianapolis on the weekends, he played in the house band of Bob McQueen's Place to Play and backed the President's Band, which featured singer Baby Leon and master of ceremonies Mr. Tee, not to be confused with the television character of television's *A-Team*. Later, he hurried down the Avenue to Al Coleman's British Lounge and performed with vocalists Aretta La Marre and Ruth Woods. Ratliff helped organize the Highlighters band, but disruptive internal politics arose and he left. He went to the Meridian Street strip, where he performed with older, more seasoned musicians at the Harem and Carousel Night Clubs. At the Harem Club, he sat in with vocalists Jimmy Guilford and Jimmy Scruggs. His aggregation included Paula Kerley Hampton Rhyne and Ronnie Rhyne alternating on drums and Tiny Adams on bass.

When Ratliff returned from the United States Air Force in 1970, he was contacted by Indiana University jazz professor and bandleader David Baker and invited to join his big band. Over the years, Ratliff has performed with a who's who of the fabled Indianapolis jazz scene, such as Jimmy Coe, Larry Liggett, Alonzo "Pookie" Johnson, Step Wharton, Reginald DuValle Jr., Willis Dyer and Russell Webster. In 1983, Ratliff participated in a jazz project that sent jazz vibrations throughout the city and country. Saxophonist Russell Webster directed a project that culminated with the release of an album entitled *Uncle Funkenstein—Together Again*. He assembled some of Indianapolis's finest jazz musicians, including Ratliff on trumpet, Claude Sifferin on piano, Melvin Rhyne on organ, Alonzo "Pookie" Johnson on saxophone, Larry Ridley on bass and James Spaulding on saxophone. Webster's mission was to redefine the concept of the Naptown sound and propel it to a higher stratosphere. Although a paltry one thousand copies were released, it was a smashing success in jazz circles around the world, and to this day, it is coveted by collectors.

Another Crispus Attucks Tiger who distinguished herself on and off Indiana Avenue was Vickie Daniel, the daughter of Mathew and Juanita Jones Daniel. She was born in Indianapolis and raised in the Lockefield Gardens Housing Development. As a small child, she was exposed to various genres of music as she walked with her mother down Indiana Avenue. She vividly remembered passing Al Coleman's British Lounge and hearing music by Lou Rawls and other musical greats. Every member of her family was a singer; her paternal grandmother sang in a female church choir in Sykeston, Missouri. During summer visits to her grandparents' home, she sat idly by listening to the sacred music while choir members rehearsed. She remembered listening to the beauty and power of the music and realizing that both secular and religious music were equal in their capacity to heal the soul and uplift the spirit. As she sat there witnessing the spectacle of the performance, she visualized an electrifying Mahalia Jackson rendering an awe-inspiring "Precious Lord" from the pulpit or a sassy Mary Wells belting out her signature tune "My Guy" from the Motown stage.

As a young child during the early 1960s, Daniel was able to get a bird's-eye view of the entertainment world courtesy of her mother, who owned and operated Juanita's Hair-Weaving Beauty Salon on the Avenue. On many occasions, she witnessed internationally and nationally known entertainers who were to perform on the Avenue stroll into her mother's shop to have their hair styled. One evening, Daniel was singing in the shop when a man entered, gingerly sat down and quietly observed her impromptu musical performance. Afterward, smiling, he approached young Daniel and encouraged her to continue singing because, in his estimation, she had a beautiful voice. She later discovered that the unknown man was J.J. Johnson, an Indianapolis-bred, internationally renowned jazz trombonist who was a veteran of the Indiana Avenue stage.

In 1968, Daniel entered Public School 23, where she was a student of Crystal Jackson and Lancaster Price. Jackson recognized her unique vocal ability and encouraged her to sing; Price taught her the basic elements of playing the flute. She continued to study the flute at Crispus Attucks under the supervision of band director William Squires. She also found time to perform as a vocalist in the Omni Band, which appeared at school functions and parties around town.

In 1977, Daniel entered Indiana University–Purdue University at Indianapolis (IUPUI) and joined the New York Street Singers. She later ventured onto Indiana Avenue and performed at various jazz clubs. Her musical mentors were Terri Hayden, Carl Hines, Hazel Johnson, Alonzo "Pookie" Johnson, Larry Liggett, Mary Moss, Russell Webster and David Young. Her musical influences were Ella Fitzgerald, Johnny Hartman, Nancy Wilson, Barbra Streisand and David Baker.

IUPUI sponsored a musical tribute to Louis Armstrong written and performed by Daniel entitled *The Smithsonian Institute's Jazz Age in Paris*. Daniel had many performances for the Indianapolis Public Library's combined literacy, visual arts and jazz poetry programs. She was accompanied by pianist Carl Hines and bassist Thomas Brinkley. She was the vocalist with the band Paradigm and performed in many of the music festivals in Indiana.

The Crispus Attucks High School Music Department produced a number of talented and accomplished musicians. For one Attucks Tiger, his music education enabled him to perform rhythm-and-blues tunes on Indiana Avenue and, later, operatic masterpieces in concert halls throughout the world. One might imagine that the distance between the smoke-filled room of George's Bar on Indiana Avenue and the bright lights and sparkling marquee above the opera house of Toronto, Canada, would be enormous, but not for one entertainer. Heretofore, the numerous entertainers who refined their craft on Indiana Avenue remained closely associated with the foundational genres of blues and jazz. Theodore Gentry's Avenue education was so all-encompassing that he transitioned to other locations and art forms with ease.

Theodore Lavelle Gentry was born on November 22, 1939, to Theodore and Dorothy Mae Logan Gentry in Indianapolis. Gentry's earliest exposure to music was provided by his mother, a vocalist with the Lavon Kemp Orchestra, which appeared at the most popular jazz clubs on the entertainment circuit. Her signature song that thrilled the crowd was "A Tisket, a Tasket," the song made famous by Ella Fitzgerald with the Chick Webb Orchestra in 1938. As a child, Gentry attended Mount Zion Baptist Church, where he sang in the choir and was immediately recognized as having a special gift.

Gentry entered Crispus Attucks High School in 1952 and became a member of the a cappella choir under the direction of Norman Merrifield. He was the principal soloist in many of the high school's musical programs. The highlight of his musical tenure at Crispus Attucks was being principal soloist in the Easter Cantata, *The Seven Last Words of Christ*, on Good Friday, March 30, 1956. After graduation, Gentry was captivated by the jazz on the Avenue and performed at George's Bar. Nightly, he packed the house, and patrons were overjoyed to hear his unique interpretations and phrasings of the current jazz standards. Gentry attended Indiana University–Bloomington from 1956 until 1958 and was drafted into the United States Army and served from 1963 to 1965.

In 1968, Gentry moved to Toronto, Canada, where he majored in music at the University of Toronto. After graduation, he obtained employment with operatic companies throughout Canada. He was a dedicated student of vocal music, constantly seeking opportunities to increase his knowledge base and gain more experience on stage. His efforts were rewarded, and he was considered by experts in the field as one of the world's finest counter tenors. A counter tenor has a male singing voice whose vocal range is equivalent to that of a contralto or, less frequently, that of a soprano. As his popularity and exposure increased, he was sought by music companies around the world.

Gentry has performed with the Toronto Symphony Orchestra, Tafemusik Baroque Orchestra, Orchestre Symphonique de Montreal, English Chamber Orchestra, Canadian Broadcasting Company, Vancouver Chamber Orchestra and National Symphony Orchestra of Washington, D.C., as well as with the National Arts Centre Orchestra, Ottawa, Canada. A concert of classical music called *A Musical Tribute to Theodore Gentry* was performed at St. George the Martyr Church, in Toronto, Canada, in 1997. He sang in German, French and Italian. Sadly, Theodore died on September 18, 2003.

One of music teacher Norman Merrifield's most outstanding students commanded the stage of the Walker Casino when she was just fourteen years old.

Hazel Elizabeth Johnson-Strong was born on January 18, 1944, to Claude and Bernice Farmer Johnson in Indianapolis. In 1949, at the tender age of five, she burst onto the local music scene, appearing on the widely popular children's program *The Talent Showcase*, which aired on WFBM television channel 6. Her introductory song was "Let Us Break Bread Together." She was accompanied on piano by her aunt Alice Wright. Young Johnson-Strong attended Robert Gould Shaw School 40 and Booker T. Washington School 17, where she received music instruction from Ruth Carter, who taught at both schools. "Miss Carter was an outstanding music teacher who was devoted and cared about every student. She really cared about your educational development," Hazel remembered. While enrolled at School 17, she was also instructed by Anderson Dailey and appeared in many of the school's musical programs.

Hazel Johnson-Strong, a jazz vocalist who performed with almost every group on the Avenue; with her husband, Mack Strong, she created a music program to train inner-city youth. *Courtesy of Mack Strong*

In 1958, upon graduation from junior high school, Johnson-Strong greatly anticipated her journey next door to Crispus Attucks High School because she had heard so many wonderful stories about its music department and outstanding choir director. "I was very excited to go to Crispus Attucks because that's where the one and only Norman Merrifield was. He was very dedicated and cared about everybody. He made sure it was right. I don't care if you had to go over the same song or phrase fifty times; he was going to continue going over it until it was right. That's the kind of teacher he was," she stated with a smile. After she entered Attucks, Hazel became involved in its music program and joined the a cappella choir and the Girls Ensemble.

During the pre-Motown days of the late 1950s, many African American female groups commanded center stage and hit the airways with rhythm-and-blues songs that gained popular acclaim from coast to coast. Foremost among these groups were the Chantels, the Shirelles and the Crystals. Their success prompted many female music students throughout the country to follow their dreams and organize groups. Johnson-Strong had a similar dream.

Darlene Newcombe, a member of Norman Merrifield's Girls Ensemble, organized a female quintet and named it the Darlatones. The group, with alternating personnel, included Hazel, Pat Wright, Carolyn Anderson, Tometta Poindexter, Jeanette Griffin and Elaine Livingston. Their signature song was "Maybe," the chart-buster released in 1957 by the Chantels, which peaked at no. 2 on the rhythm-and-blues chart and no. 15 on the popular music chart. Johnson-Strong sang lead on "Maybe," and it was a smashing success at the school's dances, talent shows and wherever they performed. The Darlatones appeared at a teen talent show at Garfield Park sponsored by the Indianapolis Parks Department and won first place. On another occasion, they sang at Northwestern Park during a bonfire shortly after a Crispus Attucks High School state championship basketball game. The young girls mounted the stage and belted out "Maybe," with Johnson-Strong's commanding alto lead, and electrified the audience. The wildly excited crowd would not permit the Darlatones to exit the stage until they performed the song several additional times.

In 1958, Johnson-Strong's aunt, Alice Wright, introduced her to popular bandleader and Indianapolis Public Schools' music supervisor, Larry Liggett, who was in search of a vocalist. After a brief audition, Liggett was so impressed with her voice quality and delivery that he hired her as the featured vocalist with his orchestra when she was only fourteen years old. Her first engagement with Liggett was at the Walker Casino, where she performed in front of hundreds of patrons. "I was scared because I hadn't performed alone in front of that many people, but it went over really well," she recalled. She stepped out on the bandstand and delivered a soulfully sweet rendition of Erroll Garner's classic jazz standard "Misty" and had the jazz patrons screaming and stomping in the aisles.

After her introductory performance on Indiana Avenue, Johnson-Strong began to travel the local entertainment circuit. She appeared at jazz hot spots such as Al Coleman's British Lounge, Flamingo Club, Paradise Bar, Place to Play and George's Bar. Later, she performed with other musical groups, such as the "Pookie" Johnson Trio, the Jimmy Coe Trio, the

Melvin Rhyne Trio and Al Coleman's Three Souls. She also sang with the original Chromatics, which featured former Harlem Globetrotter Sonny Smith on drums, David Baker on trombone and Bill Penick on saxophone. During the holiday season, Johnson-Strong performed annually at the Walker Theatre's Christmas Benefit Show. For many, this event was one of the highlights of the holiday season, as the Avenue patrons filled up the auditorium to see their favorite entertainers perform. Johnson-Strong was undoubtedly one of their favorite performers.

In 1986, Johnson-Strong founded the Indianapolis Women in Jazz program, an annual affair that showcased the talents of the many great female entertainers. Johnson-Strong realized that some of these artists did not have a proper platform on which to consistently display their talents. The primary objective of this project was to raise funds for scholarships for deserving and aspiring students of jazz, and it was extremely successful. Many of the scholarship recipients attended colleges and universities throughout the country that prepared them to become professional entertainers and music scholars.

In 1994, Johnson-Strong and her husband, Mack Strong, founded the Inner City Music School. Its primary objective was to provide music instruction for inner-city students who may not have been financially able to attend a music academy. Operating on a shoestring budget, both she and Mack worked tirelessly to raise money to fund this program and utilized personal finances to keep their project economically viable. It was reported in a news story in the *Indianapolis Star* that both Johnson-Strong and Mack literally used their own resources so the volunteer instructors would have gas money to participate in the program—now that's dedication! In honor of her many years of entertainment excellence in Indianapolis, Hazel Johnson-Strong was inducted into the Indianapolis Jazz Foundation's Hall of Fame in 2007 along with jazz great Freddie Hubbard. Also in 2008, she received the Ralph Adams Lifetime Achievement Award. Started in 2001, the Ralph Adams award honors trailblazers in the local jazz community. Hazel Johnson-Strong died on April 25, 2009, in Indianapolis.

The phrase "Chitlin' Circuit" referred to a number of performance venues throughout the eastern and southern United States from New York to Jacksonville, Florida, that were available for performances by African American musicians, comedians, dancers and other entertainers during the period of strict racial segregation in the United States. This period spanned from the early nineteenth century until the middle of the twentieth, around the mid-1960s. Indiana Avenue had long been designated as Indianapolis's stop on the Chitlin' Circuit by the *Indianapolis Recorder* and patrons on the

Avenue. During the 1940s and 1950s, one of the premier performers on this circuit was the legendary Big Maybelle.

Born Mabel Louise Smith on May 1, 1924, to Frank Smith and Alice Easley in Jackson, Tennessee, her earliest days in the music industry were spent as a soloist in the choir of her family's church. In 1932, she won first prize at the Cotton Carnival Cabaret in Memphis. Three years later, she was discovered by bandleader Dave Clark during a gospel music festival in a small church in Memphis and performed with Clark and his band. A few years later, she joined the International Sweethearts of Rhythm, an all-female interracial orchestra composed of students from Piney Woods Country Life School, Piney Woods, Mississippi. The International Sweethearts of Rhythm toured the country during World War II. In the early 1940s, before she joined the International Sweethearts of Rhythm, she was a pianist with Christine Chatman's Combo and played on its first three recordings on the Decca label in 1944. The four songs on the two records were "Bad Dream Blues/ Sad and Disappointed Jill" and "Indian River/Too Tight Ma Ma." In 1947, Big Maybelle signed a contract with the trumpeter "Hot Lips" Page's band and recorded three singles on which she was singing. "A Whole Lotta Shakin' Goin' On" was the biggest hit. Shortly thereafter, Big Maybelle appeared with Indianapolis's Joe Webb Band featuring a young John Coltrane.

During the mid-1950s, Big Maybelle entered a contract with Indianapolis's Ferguson Brothers Booking Agency, an African American entertainment promotion company, in which she agreed to perform on the Indianapolis Chitlin' Circuit. On April 7, 1956, an advertisement appeared in the *Indianapolis Recorder* announcing her appearance at Sea Ferguson's Trianon Ballroom. She also appeared at the Sunset Terrace Ballroom, Walker Casino Ballroom, the Flamingo Club, Club 16, the Pink Poodle Night Club and other entertainment establishments throughout the state. Big Maybelle developed a serious heroin problem that compromised her career in the 1960s. She died in a diabetic coma on January 23, 1972, at forty-seven years of age.

In the early 1950s, the *Indianapolis Recorder* sponsored talent shows at the Walker Theatre whose proceeds were used to provide food and clothing for needy families during the Christmas holidays. Many of the contestants seized on the opportunity to showcase their talents for a worthy cause and hoped to catch the eye of a talent scout and possibly join the ranks of the entertainers on the Chitlin' Circuit. One such entertainer was Ray Foster. Foster was born to Robert Foster Sr. and Pauline Woodard Foster on September 19, 1926, in Indianapolis, Indiana. He attended Crispus Attucks High School and served in the United States Navy during World War II. After the war, he

Ray Foster, a jazz vocalist who was a favorite at the annual *Recorder* Christmas shows, moved to New York and performed with internationally known vocalist Al Hibler in Harlem. *Courtesy of Indiana Historical Society.*

took vocal lessons at the McArthur Conservatory of Music and performed in many of the nightclubs along Indiana Avenue. His signature song was "Skylark," the popular tune penned by Hoagy Carmichael.

In the 1950s, Foster moved to New York, worked as a tailor by day and performed with internationally known vocalist Al Hibbler during the evenings at the Baby Grand Night Club in Harlem. He recorded several songs during the '70s and '80s. He was inspired by popular singer Billy Eckstein and pianist Erroll Garner, and in many of his appearances along Indiana Avenue, the audience witnessed elements of both of these entertainers. Ray Foster died March 30, 1998, in Indianapolis.

One week, there was big-band and jazz music performed in theaters and nightclubs from coast to coast, and the next week, the venues fell silent. This was during World War II, when many of the big-band and jazz musicians marched off to war. This provided an opportunity for the International Sweethearts of Rhythm, founded in 1910 by Laurence C. Jones, to capitalize on the dearth of entertainment. In the early 1920s, Jones supported Piney

Woods Country Life School by sending an all-female vocal group on the road to raise funds for its operation. This strategy proved to be successful, and in the 1940s, the International Sweethearts of Rhythm hit the road and performed at many of the Chitlin' Circuit venues that dotted the country. The African American newspaper *Chicago Defender* reported that the group was "[o]ne of the hottest stage shows that ever raised the roof of the theatre!"

George William Bright was born on November 6, 1935, to Henry Bright and Mary Eliza Simms Bright in Indianapolis. In 1941, he entered Francis W. Parker School 56, and his first music teacher was Ruth McArthur, founder, owner and instructor at the McArthur Conservatory of Music located at 808 Indiana Avenue and who was also employed by the Indianapolis Public School system. Bright enjoyed his early music education with McArthur because, according to him, "She was a demanding and no-nonsense teacher, but she was kind and we had a lot of fun in her class...I loved to play the tonette or recorder, the small flute-like instrument that we practiced our scales on."

In 1946, Bright transferred to John Hope School 26, where he was taught to play the saxophone by James Compton, and then on to Hazel Hart Hendricks School 37, where he rejoined McArthur in the music classroom and continued to study the saxophone. In 1949, Bright entered Arsenal Technical High School, enrolled in music classes and was taught by band director John White. Bright greatly anticipated the opportunity to play in a jazz band, but unfortunately, there was no jazz band in the music department. Bright sought jazz instruction and was taught by another music teacher, John O. Guynn, who had the greatest influence on his development as a tenor saxophonist. "Guynn had lived in New York and knew the woodwind scene pretty good." He knew more about jazz than anybody else, Bright recalled.

While Bright attended high school, he remembered lying in bed at night and listening to a radio jazz program broadcast from New York radio station WJZ called the *Symphony Sid Jazz Show*. This was an all-night jazz program that featured tenor saxophonist Charlie Parker, trumpeter Miles Davis, drummer Max Roach, pianist Thelonious Monk and many other jazz performers who were the most outstanding musicians in the world of jazz. "Man, I laid in that bed all night with my eyes wide-open listening to all that jazz and right then and there, I knew the musical route I wanted to travel. I got up in the morning and went to school and was half asleep all day," he reminisced. Bright later took music lessons from George Nickloff, a woodwind repairman and music teacher at the Franzman Music Company, located on Massachusetts Avenue. "Nickloff really taught me a lot and was a stickler on the basics. You had to practice your scales, and you had to do it right."

After graduation in 1956, Bright attended Indiana University for two years and joined the David Baker Big Band as a tenor saxophonist. The group performed around the Bloomington area in nightclubs and for private parties and traveled as far as the Club Shaferee located in South Bend, Indiana.

In 1960, before moving to New York, Bright played with the big bands of Lavon Kemp, Eldridge Morrison and Jimmy Coe at George's Bar, the Cotton Club and Henri's, nightclubs on Indiana Avenue. In New York, he was immediately captivated by the jazz scene. There he saw many of the performers performing live in the clubs that he had heard on the radio or seen on television or in the movies. "Man, that blew my mind seeing my idols up there on stage! At times, I had to pinch myself to make sure it was real!" Bright decided to continue his education and enrolled in the New School of Social Research located at 66 West Twelfth Street, where he majored in television production.

He met a professor at the New School who introduced him to the Beat Generation movement. "Beat Generation" referred to a group of post–World War II writers who came to prominence in the 1950s, as well as to the cultural phenomena that they both documented and inspired. Major elements of the culture of the Beat Generation included a rejection of materialism, an interest in eastern religions, optional forms of sexuality and drug experimentation. Although he was influenced by the philosophy of this movement, which dictated free expression and a rejection of the norms and mores of society, Bright continued to play traditional jazz and adhere to the performance principles of this idiom. During this period, he was also greatly influenced by prominent jazz tenor saxophonist Sonny Rollins.

Bright comically remembered standing in front of the Five Spot jazz club in the Bowery, which is the southern portion of New York City, when a long, shiny black limousine pulled up. The doors swung open, and out climbed seven-foot, one-inch National Basketball Association (NBA) superstar Wilt Chamberlain. Out on the sidewalk, he hollered, "Hey fellas, meet my little brother," and then out stepped Lew Alcindor, later known as Kareem Abdul-Jabbar, also an NBA superstar. Everyone froze in their tracks as these two basketball giants strolled through the doors into the jazz club. During the evening, Alcindor discovered that Bright was a tenor saxophonist and asked for private lessons. Bright traveled to Alcindor's house in Brooklyn to teach him the basics. Bright laughed as he remembered a funny episode in which he tried to teach Alcindor how to adjust his mouthpiece on his tenor saxophone: "Man, I had to stand on a chair to check his embouchure [mouthpiece adjustment] because he was so tall!"

In 2000, Bright returned to Indianapolis to perform at jazz clubs around town.

Chapter 14

Music Scholars and the Death of the Avenue

During the first decade of the twentieth century, when many former slaves migrated to Indianapolis, they brought with them a musical legacy that was born in the cotton fields of the Old South. Many of the "call and response" songs that the slaves sang daily as they toiled in the cotton fields also provided entertainment for them at night when they returned to their quarters. Conceivably, as they gathered to amuse themselves, these songs were accompanied by makeshift drums, banjos and any other semblance of an instrument that could be constructed. In the following decade, Ben Holliman arrived on Indiana Avenue and taught himself to play several instruments because there was no institution of music instruction available to African Americans.

However, in November 1946, that changed. Recognizing a need for music instruction of African Americans in Indianapolis, Ruth McArthur established a conservatory of music located at 808–810 Indiana Avenue. Its primary objective was to provide music instruction for African American youngsters and World War II veterans in order to fortify their appreciation of the fine arts, as well as prepare them for professional careers in the field of music. The conservatory had a band and orchestra division, which included marching and symphonic band instruction, as well as a jazz department—it was the first institution to offer a formal jazz curriculum in Indianapolis. The McArthur Conservatory was highly visible in the African American community and presented programs for various social and civic organizations.

The entertainment stars that shined so brilliantly in the Indiana Avenue constellation for several decades were not the result of a random cosmic explosion, a quirk of fate or a process of spontaneous generation. They were the proud products of men and women who worked indefatigably to ensure that their students received the best musical instruction in the land. These individuals who spent long hours of rigorous classroom instruction to polish their students' skills

Ben Holliman, a self-taught musician who played many instruments and was mentored by Russell Smith, was taken under the wing of Noble Sissle and Eubie Blake. *Courtesy of Nancy Holliman-Johnson.*

so that they could shine as brilliantly as possible were instructors at either Crispus Attucks High School or the McArthur Conservatory of Music. Who were these fantastic music educators who produced these precious jewels?

Ruth Luella McArthur was born on November 29, 1916, to Rutherford B. and Willie McArthur in Bristol, Virginia. She had one sister, Lillian, who was two years older. Her father graduated from North Carolina's Bennett College in 1904 and, eight years later, completed his medical studies at Meharry Medical College in Nashville, Tennessee.

The McArthur family moved to Indianapolis in 1926 when Dr. McArthur began his postdoctoral studies in medicine at the Indiana University School of Medicine. Ruth McArthur attended Crispus Attucks High School and graduated in 1934. Three years later, she enrolled in Tuskegee Institute and majored in band and orchestra music. Her earliest musical influence was the African American composer William Levi Dawson, who was considered the dean of African American composers. Upon completion of her bachelor's degree in music, she pursued graduate courses in musicology and chorale technique and was taught by outstanding music educators at Tuskegee Institute in Alabama. Because of World War II, she returned to Indianapolis after completing a year of graduate studies.

McArthur obtained employment as a music supervisor for the Indianapolis Public School system. She supervised the instrumental music program for more than a dozen African American elementary schools. Realizing the need to provide music education to a broader segment of the black community, McArthur began private instruction in her home. Her father, who had a medical practice in Indianapolis, had purchased a building at 808–810 Indiana Avenue in the 1940s; he deeded it to Ruth on November 11, 1955, and she opened the McArthur Conservatory of Music that same year. She sought the most credentialed personnel available to join her faculty. Among the instructors were Russell Brown and Norman Merrifield, members of the music department of Crispus Attucks High School; Lancaster Price, former music professor at Lincoln University, Jefferson City, Missouri; and Jerry Daniels, one of the original Ink Spots. Ruth McArthur died on March 1, 1994, in Detroit, Michigan.

There were two men named Brown who taught music at Crispus Attucks. The first was Harold Brown, a member of the original 1927 faculty, and the other was Russell Brown, who arrived later. Russell Wadsworth Brown was born in Philadelphia on May 25, 1908, to Domer and Esther Brown. His earliest music exposure was provided by his father, who was a barber and a musician who played the piano. His father performed in clubs and at house parties in the Philadelphia and Harrisburg, Pennsylvania areas. In 1926, Brown graduated from John Bartram High School in Philadelphia and earned his bachelor's and master's degrees in music, with the violin as his specialty, from the University of Pennsylvania and Temple University, respectively. Russell Brown financed his college education by serving in the music department of Mother Bethel African Methodist Episcopal Church.

After college, Brown auditioned as a violinist and won a seat in the Philadelphia Symphony Orchestra. He became disenchanted immediately because less qualified whites were favored by the administrators of the orchestra. Ultimately, he relinquished his seat and traveled to Wilberforce, Ohio, where he sought employment as a professor of music at Wilberforce University. After several years, he relocated to Indianapolis and began to perform as a pianist with music groups along Indiana Avenue.

Reverend Clinton Marsh of Witherspoon Presbyterian Church was in desperate need of a college-trained musician to direct his music department. He heard that there was a dynamic pianist in town and went to Indiana Avenue to locate Brown and offer him employment at his church. At first, Brown declined the offer because he was not interested in performing religious music but later reconsidered it and became the music director at Witherspoon.

Brown realized that he could not maintain himself on the paltry salary provided by the church, so he went to the Indianapolis Public School Board of Education and obtained a teaching position in the music department of Crispus Attucks High School. Brown became the director of instrumental music education and served in this capacity for more than forty years. Over that period, he taught and mentored some of the most recognized musicians in the world of music. Among his students were trombonists Reginald DuValle Jr., Locksley "Slide" Hampton and David Baker; bassists J.J. Johnson, Leroy Vinnegar and Phillip Stewart; drummers Al Coleman and Willis Kirk; tenor saxophonists Russell Webster, Bill Penick, David Young and James Spaulding; and trumpeters Virgil Jones and Clifford Ratliff. Trumpeter Freddie Hubbard and bassist Larry Ridley attended Brown's summer school music program, although they were students at Arsenal Technical and Shortridge High Schools, respectively. Russell Brown died on March 6, 1993, in Indianapolis.

Another legendary music teacher to grace the halls of Attucks was Norman LaVelle Merrifield, who was born on August 19, 1906, to Clarence and Henrietta Merrifield in Louisville. A year after his birth, his parents divorced, and his mother married John Cheatham. The family relocated to Indianapolis on July 5, 1913. In Indianapolis, Mr. Cheatham gained employment as a coal and ice deliveryman. Merrifield's family lived in a racially integrated south side community composed of hardworking residents who lived in harmony, which was rare considering the rigidly segregated housing patterns of the day. His earliest musical experience was sitting on the front porch of legendary orchestra leader Reginald DuValle Sr. at 1202 Harlan Street, watching him give a youthful and inquisitive Hoagy Carmichael music lessons. Merrifield took piano lessons from DuValle and became a gifted musician as a youngster. He observed DuValle's technique on the piano and patterned his style accordingly. Merrifield related, "This was my first piano experience." He attended Indianapolis public schools, many of which were integrated except Public School 19, which was all-black, and Public School 18, which was all-white.

He entered Arsenal Technical High School in 1920 and graduated in three years, a feat that caused a problem with the administration of the school. According to Merrifield, black students were not encouraged to excel academically, and as an example, he cited his personal case in which the administration discovered that he would graduate in a record three years and wanted to thwart his effort. He stated, "When the authorities at Arsenal Technical High School found that I was going to graduate in three years, pressure was brought to bear on one of my teachers in the annual course which was required for graduation. During the first semester, that teacher gave me straight A's. Pressure was brought because they did not want that to happen, and the second semester, I managed to skip through with a D and 2 C's."

During his high school days, Merrifield earned money by delivering the *Indianapolis Recorder* and *Indianapolis Ledger* newspapers and also assisted his father in his coal and ice delivery business. He starkly remembered the changing racial attitudes of the mid- to late 1920s. Heretofore, both black and white students attended school together in relative harmony. However, with the rise of the Ku Klux Klan and its fiery, racist leader D.C. Stephenson, the Indianapolis School Board moved to total segregation with the construction of Crispus Attucks High School. Racial tension in the community intensified, and it adversely affected his father's business. According to Merrifield, "My father's customers were, to a large extent, not necessarily Catholics, but with the impact of the Ku Klux Klan, we lost practically all of our customers except the ones who were liberal and those who were Catholics."

Merrifield entered Northwestern University in Evanston, Illinois, in 1923 and received his bachelor's degree in music education in 1927. He then traveled to Tennessee, where he taught at all-black Fisk University in Nashville for a year and at segregated Austin High School in Knoxville for three years. Merrifield left Tennessee and returned to Northwestern, where he earned his master's degree in music education. From there, he went on to Florida Agricultural & Mechanical College for Blacks, where he served as dean of the College of Music. Being a proud person and not willing to accept the indignities of American racism that he experienced daily in the South, Merrifield returned to Indianapolis in 1933 and taught at Crispus Attucks until his retirement in 1967. During World War II, he attended Army Band School in Arlington, Virginia, and then was shipped to France, Belgium and Germany, where he saw hostile action. He married Estelle Perry in 1943, and they had one son, Norman Merrifield Jr. Norman Merrifield died on February 3, 1997, in Indianapolis.

LaVerne Edward Newsome, the third of the excellent Crispus Attucks music instructors, performed for many years with the Indianapolis Symphonic Band. He was born on October 21, 1907, to Edward and Cora Newsome in Elgin, Illinois, and was trained as a classical violinist at the Northwestern University School of Music, where he earned a bachelor's degree in music education and a master's of music and violin performance. He began his teaching career as an instructor of violin and school music at historically black Talladega College in Alabama from 1929 until 1937. He came to Indianapolis in 1937 to become teacher, orchestra director and chairman of the music department at Crispus Attucks, where he remained for thirty-seven years.

On June 15, 1940, Newsome married Maenell Hamlin in Indianapolis and left two years later to serve in the military. From 1942 until 1945, during World War II, he served in the Ninety-second Infantry "Buffalo Division" in Italy. When he returned, he performed with the Philharmonic Orchestra of Indianapolis from 1947 until 1992. In 1975, after retiring from Crispus Attucks, he founded the LaVerne Edward Newsome String Ensemble, and in 1979, he organized and coordinated the *Music Stars of Tomorrow*, an annual recital for advanced high school and middle school student musicians. Wabash College in Crawfordsville, Indiana, awarded him an honorary doctorate of humane letters on May 13, 2001, in recognition of his outstanding contributions to the cultural life of the Indianapolis community. LaVerne Newsome died on August 25, 2001, in Indianapolis.

The demise of Indiana Avenue was a slow and agonizing ordeal. Like a beautiful flower existing in hot, stagnant air under an unforgiving sun, Indiana Avenue withered and died a painful death. At one time, there was a booming "world within a world," where a person could buy groceries, fill a prescription, get her hair done or his hair cut, obtain a shoe shine, attend the theater, have dinner, visit a doctor and/or pay last respects at a funeral home without ever leaving the Avenue. By 1970, the Avenue was a negligible shadow of its former glory.

Gone were the laughter and merriment of neatly attired high-stepping music lovers prancing down the Avenue in cadence with the sounds of the blues and jazz escaping from the Cotton Club. The hustle and bustle of everyday people hurrying to and fro enjoying the ambiance and the warm handshakes and sincere hugs given and received by good folks happy to see one another gradually disappeared. Indiana Avenue would never regain its former glory.

According to *Polk's Business Directory*, which listed businesses and residents of the Indiana Avenue area, there were 332 businesses there in 1930. Many of the businesses were listed as soft drink establishments, a label that was a cover for illegal alcohol sales, which generated other illegal activities such as prostitution, drugs and gambling. Indiana Avenue had begun to hemorrhage by 1960, with only 83 business establishments listed. By 1970, the number had been reduced to 78. In 2010, there were only 20 businesses in the Indiana Avenue area.

Businesses left the area for three principal reasons: illegal activities, highway construction and urban renewal. Among the initial causes of the commercial decline was vice in the forms of gambling and illegal liquor. As longtime Indiana Avenue resident Thomas Ridley remembered, "Gambling was always a big deal on the Avenue, and it really escalated after World War II. Many of the liquor stores fronted for gambling operations, and the Avenue began to go down slowly. Many of the wealthier black middle-class folks stopped frequenting the Avenue because of this change."

At the turn of the twentieth century, when segregation was the law of the land, business enterprises and life in general were booming on Indiana Avenue. African Americans could not patronize most white downtown department stores, theaters, restaurants and other businesses and were forced to exist and circulate their money in their "world within a world." The downtown L.S. Ayres Department Store tearoom was a case in point. African Americans were employed in the kitchen and among the custodial staff but could not be received as patrons. Interestingly, former African American employees remembered that there was an unwritten profile of individuals who were served there: middle-aged, socially mobile white women wearing hats and necklaces, with long gloves up to their elbows. Some of the segregation policies began to tumble in the 1940s and 1950s as African American patrons began to frequent white-owned entertainment establishments in other areas of the city. Many had gotten better-paying jobs and longed to enjoy new social experiences. As the "Black Dollar," which had circulated and recirculated on Indiana Avenue since before the Civil War, began to disappear, buildings fell into disrepair, entertainment decreased and some clubs closed.

Another factor that weighed heavily on the demise of Indiana Avenue was the expansion of the federal interstate highway system. In the September 2, 1972 edition of the *Indianapolis News* daily newspaper, there appeared an article titled "Interstate Seventy Shaping Up on the Westside." It contained a panoramic, aerial view of the effects of the highway system on the west side of Indianapolis, including Indiana Avenue. One could clearly observe that this construction process would directly affect and constitute a destabilizing factor on Indiana Avenue. An entire neighborhood east of Indiana Avenue near Crispus Attucks High School was completely demolished. Many of the churches that served as anchors in the community, such as Mount Zion and Mount Paran Baptist Churches, had to relocate because of the coming interstate. Simultaneously, there was an urban renewal project that had been planned many years before that had as its primary objective the expansion of the Indiana University Downtown Extension. Steps were taken to acquire as much property as possible adjacent to Indiana Avenue, including the

Lockefield Gardens Housing Development. A great neighborhood debate ensued in which residents courageously fought the trustees of Indiana University to maintain their homes. After years of struggle, Indiana University reigned victorious, and hundreds of residents were relocated to other parts of the city to accommodate a larger Indiana University–Purdue University campus.

One hundred years from now, historians and scholars will glance back to the twentieth century and ask many questions. Who were these people who inhabited Indiana Avenue? What were their dreams and aspirations? What contributions did they make for the betterment of Indianapolis? How did they survive? What is their legacy? These debatable and intriguingly perplexing questions may puzzle scholars for many years. However, from a historical perspective, some answers may be as follows.

Indiana Avenue was a destination point for many escaped and ex-slaves in the nineteenth century who sought refuge in a "Promised Land" called Indianapolis. With little more than the shirts on their backs and a few bread crumbs in their pockets, they came to this city in search of freedom, justice and equality. They labored for many years to create the Avenue, with its booming commercial enterprise that employed hundreds of folks who were fiercely independent and extremely proud to call Indianapolis their home. Later, this commercial enterprise developed into an entertainment empire that dispatched jazz and entertainment emissaries to the four corners of the earth and won the Avenue international acclaim.

Some music historians, and in particular New Orleans's musician/historian trumpeter Wynton Marsalis, continually insist that New Orleans is the sole birthplace of jazz and other music genres. They often cite cornetist/bandleader King Oliver, saxophonist/clarinetist/composer Sidney Bechet, pianist Jelly Roll Morton and trumpeter Louis Armstrong to substantiate their argument. However, conventional historic thought would take issue with this assessment. Jazz and other music genres were art forms derived from traditional music produced in the Congo of central Africa. Many of these Congolese slaves shipped to this country also brought these music genres with them. During the period of slavery, they were transported to the plantations of many cities across the southern United States in addition to New Orleans. Therefore, one might logically conclude that wherever they were transported, they carried their musical traditions to these parts of the country.

Jazz and other music genres may have one of its points of origin in New Orleans; however, Indiana Avenue musicians such as the Ink Spots, Noble

Sissle, Ben Holliman, Reginald DuValle, Bill Jennings, Wes Montgomery, Buddy Montgomery, Monk Montgomery, Freddie Hubbard, Leroy Vinnegar, J.J. Johnson, Carl Perkins, Slide Hampton, Willis Kirk, Jimmy Coe, Erroll Grandy, David Young, Al Coleman, Beryl Steiner, Melvin Rhyne, David Baker, Larry Ridley, Phil Ranelin, James Spaulding, Mingo Jones, Al Finnell and Virgil Jones were products of the Indiana Avenue mystique that transformed jazz and other genres of music and took them to a higher stratosphere. Wherever African Americans called home, there was jazz.

Down Indiana Avenue, this tantalizing boulevard of excitement and entertainment, strolled some of the greatest entertainment personalities ever produced in America. They left the Avenue relatively unknown and traveled around the world displaying their rich entertainment heritage. The remains of the once proud Indiana Avenue are sparse, with only the Madam Walker Theatre Center, a portion of Lockefield Gardens and the jazz sculptures created by John Spaulding serving as a reminder of the past. Although the problems of gambling, dope, prostitution, illegal alcohol and other vices plagued this community in its latter years and sullied its reputation, the spirit and determination of those honest, hardworking Americans who once inhabited this hallowed ground shall live forever.

Bibliography

Bodenhamer, David J., and Robert G. Barrows. *The Encyclopedia of Indianapolis*. Bloomington: Indiana University Press, 1994.

Carmichael, Hoagy. *The Stardust Road*. Bloomington: Indiana University Press, 1983.

Ferguson, Earline Rae. "A Community Affair: African-American Women's Club Work in Indianapolis, 1879–1917." PhD diss., Indiana University, 1997.

Gatewood, Willard B. *Aristocrats of Color: The Black Elite, 1880–1920*. Bloomington: Indiana University Press, 1990.

———. *Slave and Freeman: The Autobiography of George Knox*. Bloomington: Indiana University Press, 1990.

Goldberg, Marvin. *More than Words Can Say*. New York: Scarecrow Press, 1998.

Gray, Ralph D. *IUPUI: The Making of an Urban University*. Bloomington: Indiana University Press, 2003.

Kimball, Robert, and William Bolcom. *Reminiscing with Sissle and Blake*. New York: Viking Press, 1973.

Piatt Dunn, Jacob. *Greater Indianapolis: The History, the Industries, the Institutions, and the People of a City of Homes*. Chicago: Lewis Publishing Company, 1910.

Schiedt, Duncan. *The Jazz State of Indiana*. Indianapolis: Indiana Historical Society, 1977.

Sudhalter, Richard. *Stardust Melody*. New York: Oxford University Press, 2002.

Thornbrough, Emma Lou. *The Negro in Indiana Before 1900*. Indianapolis: Indiana Historical Society Collections, 1957.

Warren, Stanley. *Hail to the Green, Hail to the Gold*. Virginia Beach, VA: Donning Company Publishers, 1998.

Williams, David L. "Alphonso Young: Taking Jimi Hendrix to 'School.'" *Indianapolis Eye News*, June 30, 2003.

———. "The Ferguson Brothers and Indiana Avenue." *Traces* (Summer 2007).

———. "Remembering the Foster Hall Quartet: A Nearly Forgotten Nugget of Indianapolis' Black History." *Indianapolis Eye News*, February 2, 2004.

INTERVIEWS

Appleton, Otis "Killer Ray." Telephone interview, December 1, 2008.

Bacon, Trevor, Jr. Personal interview, June 19, 2011.

Baker, David. Telephone interview, August 14, 2011.

Barker, Charles, and Shirley Barker. Personal interview on Bryant A. "Buddy" Hurd, June 13, 2011.

———. Personal interview on the Buddy Bryant Orchestra, May 30, 2011.

Barth, Benny. Telephone interview, May 21, 2011.

Blanchard, Johnny. Personal interview, May 1, 2011.

Boyd, Rozelle. Personal interview on William "Bill" Boyd, June 7, 2012.

Bright, George. Personal interview, August 13, 2011.

Bush, Linda. Personal interview on Aretta La Marre and Chuck Bush, June 13, 2011.

Campbell, James. Personal interview on William Leroy Jennings, June 1, 2012.

———. Personal interview on William Thomas "Champion Jack," July 13, 2011.

Childs-Helton, Sally. Personal interview on Robert Duncan, June 11, 2010.

Coe, Jimmy, Jr. Personal interviews on Jimmy Coe, March 13, 2011, and May 13, 2009.

Coleman, Al. Personal interview on Alonzo "Pookie" Johnson, David Young, Dickie Laswell, Erroll "Hound Dog" Grandy, James "Step" Wharton, Leroy Vinnegar, Merrill Laswell, Thomas "Buddy" Parker and Willis Dyer, March 16, 2007.

Cumberland, Ray. Personal interview, June 1, 2011.

Daniel, Vickie. Personal interview, May 1, 2010.

Dickinson, Dick. Telephone interview, June 18, 2011.

DuValle, Reginald, III. Personal interview on Reginald DuValle Jr., March 18, 2009.

Finnell, Al. Personal interview, May 1, 2013.

Fowlkes-Norfleet, Betty. Personal interview on Eugene Fowlkes, June 21, 2011.

Garvin, Flo. Telephone interview on Ophelia Hoy, May 1, 2010.

Gurnell-Ayers, Marietta. Personal interview on Carl Bailey, July 23, 2009.

Hampton, Locksley Wellington "Slide." Telephone interview, December 1, 2013.

Hampton, Paula. Telephone interview on the Hampton family, June 20, 2011.

Hardiman, David. Telephone interview, May 1, 2011.

Holliman-Johnson. Personal interview on Ben Holliday, June 1, 2012.

Johnson, Beverly (Debbie Andrews). Personal interview, January 23, 2010.

———. Personal interview on Robert "Sonny" Johnson, July 3, 2011.

Johnson, Kevin. Personal interview on J.J. Johnson, June 12, 2011.

Jones, Mingo. Personal interview, June 2, 2012.

Karim, Wali, and Ronald Foster. Personal interview on Ray Foster, November 17, 2013.

Kirk, Willis. Telephone interview, May 18, 2011.

Leggett-Davidson, Valerie. Personal interview on Larry Liggett, June 18, 2011.

McDaniels-Heath, Marla. Telephone interview on James "Jimmy" McDaniels, May 13, 2011.

McLawler, Sarah. Telephone interview, July 11, 2010.

Parham, Darlene. Telephone interview on Count Fisher, March 18, 2009.

Penick, Bill. Telephone interview, May 1, 2011.

Perkins, Freddie. Telephone interview on Carl Perkins, March 16, 2010.

Pierson, Richard. Personal interview on the Four Thunderbolts, June 1, 2013.

Price, Lancaster, and Ellen Price-Sayles. Personal interview, August 12, 2011.

Ranelin, Phillip. Telephone interview, July 20, 2012.

Ratliff family. Personal interview on Noble Sissle, April 18, 2012.

Ratliff, Clifford. Personal interview, February 10, 2011.

Rhyne, Melvin. Personal interview, June 12, 2011.

Ridley, Larry. Telephone interview, June 12, 2011.

———. Telephone interview on Ted Dunbar, August 1, 2011.

———. Telephone interview on William "Monk" Montgomery, June 1, 2011.

Ridley, Tom. Personal interview on Michael Ridley and the Russell Smith Orchestra, April 11, 2010.

Schiedt, Duncan. Personal interview on Francis "Scrapper" Blackwell, April 14, 2011.

———. Personal interview on Leroy Carr and Wheeler "Doc" Montgomery, January 12, 2011.

Shacklett, Johnny. Telephone interview, July 13, 2012.

Spaulding, James. Telephone interview, June 1, 2011.

Steiner, Bill. Telephone interview on Beryl William Steiner, June 1, 2011.

Stephens, Billy. Personal interview on Alec Stephens, August 14, 2011.

Strong, Mack, and Hazel Johnson-Strong. Personal interview, May 13, 2011.

Taylor-Carr, Carolyn. Telephone interview on Leslie William "Bear" Taylor, May 7, 2010.

Taylor, John. Personal interview on James "Yank" Rachell, August 13, 2010.

Walker, Ruth, and Sheila Turner-Cooper. Personal interview on Theodore Gentry, June 21, 2012.

Webster, Lexie. Telephone interview on Russell Webster, May 1, 2010.

Wimberley, Marcia, and Nathan Wimberley. Personal interview on Virgil Jones, June 13, 2012.

Womack, Bob, Jr. Personal interview on Bob Womack, March 7, 2011.

Woods, Henry. Personal interview on the Brown Buddies, December 1, 2011.

Index

About the Author

David Leander Williams is a collector of memorabilia, historical artifacts and information about African American history, particularly slavery and African American music history. He has used his vast knowledge to write a book about the entertainment empire that developed on Indiana Avenue from its beginnings in 1821 until its demise in the 1970s. Williams is a person of many talents and interests—African/Middle Eastern political history, Brazilian slave history, foreign languages (his collegiate undergraduate major was Spanish and Portuguese literature, and he had to be

Author David Leander Williams attired in the traditional national dress of Nigeria. *Author's collection.*

proficient in Arabic for his graduate school program), biology, medicine and music production. His first love, however, is music. He holds bachelor's and master's degrees, but more importantly, he attended and graduated from Crispus Attucks High School, an institution that figures so prominently in this book. Williams personally knows many of the musicians about whom he writes. There has been very little written about the history of African Americans in Indianapolis and even less by an African American. That makes *Indianapolis Jazz* an important book for all Hoosiers who want to know more about their history. It will also be a vital supplementary text for Indiana middle school/high school/university history classes. This book uncovers the hidden and sometimes painful experiences of a people who triumphed against all odds—a people who grew stronger as the magnitude of oppression and adversity grew larger.

Visit us at
www.historypress.net
....
This title is also available as an e-book